Working with Americans:

A practical guide for Asians on how to succeed with U.S. managers

by

Joel Wallach
Gale Metcalf

With Best Compliments.

Bangalore 28/1/2003

Working with Americans:

A practical guide for Asians on how to succeed with U.S. managers

by

Joel Wallach
Gale Metcalf

McGRAW-HILL BOOK CO.

Singapore	Auckland	Bogotá	Caracas
Lisbon	London	Madrid	Mexico
Milan	Montreal	New Delhi	New York
Paris	San Juan	San Francisco	St Louis
Sydney	Tokyo	Toronto	

WORKING WITH AMERICANS: A PRACTICAL GUIDE FOR ASIANS ON HOW TO SUCCEED WITH U.S. MANAGERS

7 8 9 0 BJ FC LG 9 8

Editor: W.L.Lam

Library of Congress Cataloging-in-Publication Data

Wallach, Joel, 1947-
    Working with Americans : a practical guide for Asians on how to succeed with U.S. managers / by Joel Wallach, Gale Metcalf.
       p.   cm.
    Includes index.
    ISBN 0-07-113838-2
    1. Industrial management--Social aspects--United States.
2. Corporate culture--United States. 3. Asians--Employment--United States. 4. Cross-cultural orientation--Asia. 5. Intercultural communication--Asia. I. Metcalf, Gale. 1947-   II. Title.
H070.U5W25   1995
302.3'5--dc20

                94-34947
                CIP

When ordering this title, use ISBN 0-07-113838-2

Printed in Singapore

About the Authors

Joel Wallach and Gale Metcalf have lived and worked in East and Southeast Asia for more than fifteen years. They have consulted with the U.S. government and more than 100 international companies on issues of preparing both American and Asian staff to work effectively in the international workplace.

The authors, a husband and wife team, currently reside in Taipei where they provide cross-cultural training for Americans going to Asia as well as for Asians working with American multinational companies or relocating to the U.S.

Table of Contents

Preface

Working With Americans is a practical guide for those who want to succeed in working with managers from the United States. It offers concrete suggestions on how to be more effective when working with Americans. This book should prove helpful to:

- Asian managers and administrative staff working with American managers in Pacific Rim countries.
- Asian managers assigned to the U.S.A.
- Asian managers who deal with an American home office or with visiting American consultants.
- Recent immigrants from Asia to the U.S.A.
- Asian students in business management training programs.
- American managers who want to increase their cross-cultural effectiveness when working with Asian clients, colleagues, superiors and subordinates.

This book grew out of more than ten years of experience designing and conducting orientation programs for Westerners relocating to Asia. Over time, executives of American multinational companies, seeing the value of cross-cultural briefings for the American manager relocating to Asia, asked us to develop and conduct similar programs for Asian managers who were being transferred to the U.S. Not long after that, numbers of American and Asian executives came to us to request another program. They saw a critical need for cross-cultural training for the Asian manager who wasn't going anywhere, but who still had to deal with foreigners who had very different cultural ideas and behaviors. From this a training program, *East Meets West*, was born, which has served more than 600 Asian managers over the last four years.

We began to develop the cross-cultural training program for Asian managers (and this book) by conducting many hundreds of interviews with Asian and American managers. We asked the simple question, "Tell us about experiences in which you interacted with an American (or alternatively, an Asian) in which you ended up feeling confused, embarrassed, annoyed or unsure as to the best way to respond." From their answers came a pattern of issues and areas in which Asians and Americans, even those with the best of intentions, misunderstood each other. The result was they felt frustrated and less effective than when dealing with colleagues from their own culture.

This book is not about all Americans, or even about all working Americans. It is about American managers. Of course, American managers, like Asian managers, are not all the same. There is no such thing as a "typical American manager". American management has changed considerably in the last few decades. It is becoming more diverse, as increasing numbers of women, African-Americans (black Americans), Hispanics (Spanish-speaking Americans) and Asian-Americans become part of the management team.

We believe that there are some identifiable, traditional messages about what it takes to be successful in American business. These are messages which most Americans in management today have received, whether they are white males, women or members of minority groups. They have gotten these messages in their companies, in business schools, in their early working lives, or just growing up in American society. To a great extent, these traditional ways of looking at, and responding to, the world of work still determine how people are expected to act and interact at work. For this reason, they form the core of this book. They, of course, are generalizations. Nevertheless, it has been our experience that they provide a useful starting point for gaining a better understanding of the thinking, behavior, and values which have influenced, and which continue to influence, the behavior of Americans in business. As America changes, these cultural messages on how to be successful and effective will also change.

Likewise, it is neither easy nor accurate to talk about all Asian cultures as if they were one. Japanese are very different from Indonesians. Thais are very different from Koreans. Yet, there are some commonalities among all Asian societies of the Pacific Rim which allow for generalizations to be made when comparing them with American society. Much of what we say about Asians is based on our own experience when working in East and Southeast Asia. At the same time, we have consulted numbers of works on the cultures of the region in search of those common cultural characteristics that span the societies of the Pacific Rim.

In the interests of readability, we have not qualified the terms "Asians" and "Americans" with such words as "most", " many", "the majority", every time they are used in the book. The Asian reader knows that no statement of behavior or cultural characteristic holds true for all Asians. The American reader knows this is also the case when talking about Americans. What needs to be kept in mind (and fought against) throughout the book is the natural tendency to see people from one's own culture as unique and highly distinct and people from a different, more foreign, culture as all the same. Cultural generalizations, as hypotheses for explaining and predicting behavior, can be most helpful; stereotyping, or seeing all people from a culture or a region as the same, limits one's view and minimizes the ability to see and to deal with the diversity which truly exists. If the reader remembers that exceptions are likely to be found for every idea presented in this book, then he or she will not fall into the trap of stereotyping or seeing all Americans (or all Asians) as the same.

Each author is inevitably a product of his or her culture and experience and sees the world from that unique perspective. As such, readers need to remember that others writing about cross-cultural topics in the field of business may have chosen to emphasize different points or to interpret them in different ways. Other topics may have been included or ideas we have included, left out. Our primary goal in writing this book has been to encourage managers to think about cross-cultural differences, to provide some background to help explain cultural differences which exist between Asians and Americans in the work setting, and to suggest some practical guidelines for behavior which will make the Asian reader more effective in working with American colleagues.

This book is only half of what needs to be done. While Asians can benefit from better understanding Americans, Americans, in turn, need to understand and appreciate the cultural traditions which have made Asia the most dynamic and exciting marketplace in the world today. It is our hope that this book, in addition to assisting Asians working with American managers, will begin to inform the culturally-sensitive American manager of the areas of cross-cultural differences which exist when working with his or her Asian colleagues. By each and every manager learning about and understanding his or her own culture as well as the culture of his or her colleagues, we can maximize the opportunities that are opening up for all of us in our increasingly global world.

Joel Wallach
Gale Metcalf

Acknowledgements

Writing a book about cross-cultural differences is an effort of literally hundreds of people. We would like to express our appreciation to the many Asian and American businessmen and businesswomen who helped us to identify the critical issues that form the basis of this book. The hundreds of participants who attended our cross-cultural training programs over the last few years further helped us to identify issues and taught us ways of presenting them in an orderly, logical manner.

We would be remiss if we did not express our appreciation to some special friends and colleagues who assisted us in the editing of this book. In particular, we would like to thank Jon Allen, Betty Atherton, C.K. Chen, David Fuller, Michelle Green, Bob and Deborah Hefferon, Loretta Jones-Wilson, Eva Salazar-Liu and Bob Wallach for reading parts of the manuscript and making valuable recommendations on how it could be improved. Special thanks goes to Fred Kerner who advised us on the publication process as well as W.L. Lam our editor, who with great patience and support helped us through the book's birthing process.

A special word of thanks goes to our teenage son, Josh, for his willingness to listen to endless discussions about this project. We have appreciated his humor and support throughout.

With all the help and advice we have received from so many people, this book is, indeed, a joint effort. Any errors or omissions, however, are purely the responsibility of the authors.

Section I: Foundations for Understanding Americans at Work

1

Culture at Work

The Global Manager: Working Effectively with Different Cultures

Mr. Hiro becomes withdrawn when a portion of a report he worked on is criticized by an American colleague in a staff meeting. He feels he is being criticized personally. His colleague, Mr. Price, isn't even aware he has hurt his feelings and is puzzled at the change of behavior in Mr. Hiro and what he interprets as an "uncooperative" attitude.

Mr. Chiang has worked very hard on a project assigned by his new American supervisor, Mr. Santini. He stays late, brings work home, and does the best he can. Mr. Santini doesn't seem to notice this extra effort. Mr. Chiang feels unappreciated for his display of loyalty and hard work for the company. Mr. Santini is aware of the extra hours, but looks to increased market share as what really counts, and he hasn't seen any changes yet.

"Cross-cultural missing"

What do these situations have in common? They show the high potential for either or both the Asian and American manager to leave a situation feeling frustrated, annoyed, confused or embarrassed. They have just experienced what we call "cross-cultural missing".

Cross-cultural missing (misunderstanding) is what happens when two people from two different cultures,

3

both with the best of intentions, trying to work together harmoniously, somehow find themselves in a situation where they feel out of control, frustrated, confused or ineffective. The result is that people's feelings get hurt, the work doesn't get done, and it becomes even harder the next time around to work with someone from that culture.

When things don't go right when you are working with someone from a culture different from your own, there is a good chance that you are experiencing a cross-cultural miss. Are these misunderstandings inevitable? Probably so. Nevertheless, they can be minimized, if not avoided completely. This means the damage to good working relationships can be reduced and the chance of getting the job done effectively can be increased.

Cultural differences can be a source of stress

When things are going well at work, cultural differences are items of interest, good for dinner table conversation, adding spice and diversity to the workplace. It's easy to be flexible when few demands are placed upon you. However, when stress is added to the mix — tight timelines, difficult negotiations, budgets under pressure, sales or production targets not being met — the situation changes very quickly. Unless they are acknowledged and addressed, cultural differences can become a source of stress which make getting the job done even harder.

To be a successful manager today, you need to be able to work effectively with people who come from other cultures. Asians need to understand Americans; Americans need to understand Asians; and both need to learn more about Europeans, Latins, Africans, Arabs and others. To be a winner in the international business environment of today and tomorrow, every manager will need to add a new set of skills to his or her job description. Those are the skills of cross-cultural effectiveness — being able to work successfully with people who come from backgrounds very different from their own.

Culture's Impact

Our culture determines our behavior

It is often said that we are products of our culture. This means that a large part of how we behave and what we believe comes from the influences of the people, institutions, and thinking that surrounds us as we are growing up. What we say when we greet someone, what we eat for dinner, what we talk about and what not to talk about with new acquaintances, even how far apart we stand when conversing, are all behaviors that we learn from our culture. The culture of any given society allows people in that society to interact fairly easily by providing guidelines or rules for what is and what is not normal and expected. Culture provides the "social oil" for smooth interactions between people. Without it, we would not be able to function. We would have to think about and decide on each of the thousands of choices about how to behave as we interact with others daily.

Initially, we learn our culture from our family. The stories your grandmother told you, the look of approval from your father for how you acted towards guests in your home, the constant reminders from your mother about how to be polite, the way you saw your parents and older family members behave, are all ways that your culture was taught to you as a child. As we grow older, our culture continues to influence us through our friends, school and our religion. TV, radio and newspapers also play a part. In both direct and indirect ways, we are guided to look at and to deal with the world from the perspective of our culture. To put it simply, our culture provides us with a "set of rules" for how to behave and a "set of glasses" for how to see and interpret the world.

Culture: A "set of rules"

Often, when two individuals from different cultures work or socialize together, they soon discover that some of their cultural rules differ. They have been taught different ways to act in the same situation. Let's look at the simple example of deciding what time to arrive for an appointment. If you have a business meeting set for

10 a.m., the rules of American culture expect that you will arrive a few minutes before 10 a.m. so that you will be ready to begin the meeting exactly at ten. If you are going to be more than a few minutes late, it is expected that you will call to inform your colleague. If you are invited to a social appointment, say dinner at the home of an American for 7 p.m., it is culturally expected that you would arrive ten to fifteen minutes later than the scheduled time. If you arrive earlier than 7 p.m., it is likely that you will embarrass the host or hostess as he or she will not be ready to receive you. If you're more than twenty minutes late, you are expected to apologize for your tardiness. If you're more than one half hour late, you are expected to have a very good reason and to be very apologetic. Almost all Americans know these cultural rules for business and social appointments and they follow them most of the time. These are very different cultural rules from those that exist in many Asian societies. Clearly, the potential for cross-cultural missing is great.

Another example: Mr. Sompoerno from Indonesia is invited to the home of his American boss for dinner. The meal is served American-style, with initial portions placed on each person's plate by the hostess. When Mr. Sompoerno is almost finished with his serving, the American hostess asks whether he would like "seconds", meaning, would he like more food. Mr. Sompoerno, not wanting to appear impolite, says "no", expecting that, according to the rules of his culture, the hostess will ask two or three more times, after which it would be polite to accept more food. The American hostess doesn't ask again, assuming that if Mr. Sompoerno wanted more, he would have taken more food when asked. Mr. Sompoerno goes away from the table still hungry. Operating with different cultural rules can make being a good host and being a good guest quite complicated!

Cultural rules at work

When you go to work, you carry your cultural rules with you. They provide guidelines for how to do your job, how to interact with colleagues and how to make and implement decisions. They influence choices about how to motivate staff, how to deal with conflict, how to conduct and participate in business meetings, when, how, and if to give your boss "bad news".

Culture: A "set of glasses"

In addition to a set of rules, your culture provides you with a "set of glasses". Your culture serves as a filter or lens through which you see and interpret the world. Think about it this way. If you look at a painting through a pair of dark sunglasses, it will look different than if you put on your reading glasses (or your father's eyeglasses!) to see it. What is different each time is not the painting, but your view of it, which is affected by the glasses you wear. When we say that our culture provides us with a set of glasses, we mean that it has taught us how to look at things, how to interpret and make sense out of the world. Our cultural glasses can limit what we see. At times, they also cause us to see the same thing quite differently from someone of another culture.

Try this quick puzzle. See if you can connect all nine dots below in four straight lines *without* picking your pen or pencil up from the page.

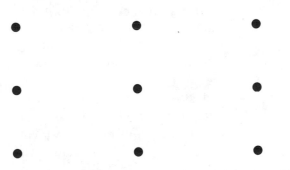

If you found it difficult, don't be discouraged. Most people were not able to figure this out the first time they tried it. The critical question for us to examine is why this puzzle was difficult. The answer (see page 24) is that most people try to solve the problem by staying within the box they imagine around the dots. However, the puzzle can't be done unless you go outside of this imagined box.

Just like the box you put around the nine dots, the culture you grow up in defines and puts limits on how you see the world. For example, what we think of as food — what is and is not acceptable to eat — is determined by our culture. Most Japanese will perceive sushi as a tasty delicacy; many Americans will see the same thing as uncooked fish, not yet ready to eat. Many Chinese will enjoy chicken feet along with their rice; most Americans view chicken feet as a part of the chicken to be thrown away, not eaten. Generally, Southeast Asians love the smell of ripe durians; Americans catching a whiff of the same scent, may question whether they've gotten too close to an open sewer. Alternatively, many Americans like the taste of blue cheese, while many Asians find the smell most unpleasant. People of different cultures have very different reactions to the same things. The difference is the cultural glasses or filters through which they see the world.

Our language reflects our culture

Our language is an important part of our culture and a reflection of what our culture sees as important. Looking at the words we use can give us some idea of the way culture influences our ability to "see" things. For example, for Americans, there is only one word for rice. To describe different types of rice using English, you have to add additional, descriptive words to explain what you mean (i.e rice in the field, unhusked rice, rice cooked with coconut milk). In Malay (and in many other Asian languages), there are many single words to describe rice in its different varieties and states (i.e. *nasi, pulut, beras, padi*). Because the Malay language distinguishes these differences so clearly and easily, people from the Malay culture see differences when looking at rice that an American may never notice. It is their cultural glasses which allow them to see these differences.

Rice is but one example of the different ways our language teaches us what to look for, what is important. Most Asian languages have many words to identify different members of the family — older brother, younger sister, uncle on the father's side, etc. The words provide much more detail than comparable English words. Many Asian languages also have different vocabulary for people of higher, equal or lower status. It's no wonder that people from Asian cultures are more aware of, and sensitive to, differences in status and position than many of their American counterparts. Their cultural glasses, developed through their language and other cultural influences, train them from an early age to pay attention to these differences. Americans are not nearly as good at seeing differences in relationships which Asians are taught to see from birth. Their cultural glasses have not trained them to be as sensitive to these differences.

Cultural glasses at work

Of course, you bring your cultural glasses with you to work. There, they help define and influence how you see such issues as what is a good employee, what is a good boss, what is an appropriate working relationship with a colleague or a contractor, even the definition of success at work. Being clear on both your culture's glasses and rules, as well as those of your American counterparts, will provide you with valuable information on how to succeed in today's multi-cultural workplace.

Cultural Differences Make a Difference

Culture is like an iceberg

Imagine, if you will, an iceberg — that big block of ice that floats in the ocean and can pose such danger to ships. About 10 percent, the tip of the iceberg, lies above the surface and can easily be seen. The other 90 percent lies below the surface, unseen. This is what causes shipwrecks. As numbers of authors (Levine, Baxter & McNulty, 1987) writing about cross-cultural issues suggest, culture is like an iceberg. The parts which you can easily see are like the tip of the iceberg. If you are a good cultural observer, you will be careful not to crash there.

How to greet someone, the use of business cards, how to dress for the office, how and what to drink at a business dinner are all examples of cultural differences that are easy to observe and learn about. These differences often relate to social etiquette, the do's and don'ts, the customs and traditions which are relatively easy to observe. Usually, they are not the cause of the most serious cross-cultural problems.

Culture is like an iceberg

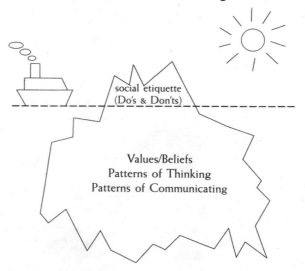

social etiquette
(Do's & Don'ts)

Values/Beliefs
Patterns of Thinking
Patterns of Communicating

Below the surface: Values, thinking, communicating

Most of an iceberg is hidden from view, deep under the sea. Just as it is the submerged part of the iceberg that causes shipwrecks, it is the hidden part of culture that causes us the most problems when we try to work with someone from another culture. What lies beneath the surface are the values and beliefs of our culture, what our culture tells us is important, as well as the ways of thinking and communicating which our culture teaches us. Values and beliefs are significant because they form the basis for our decisions and actions. We act based upon what's important to us. What is important has been learned largely through our culture, at a very early age. The way we think and the way we communicate, while seeming perfectly natural and "normal", are also taught to us by our culture. This means that people from very different cultures are not only likely to have different values but, also, to communicate and to think very differently from each other. It is often these "below the surface" differences, hidden from view, which cause "shipwrecks" in cross cultural relationships.

Consider the following moral problem:

You are on a ship with your spouse, your mother and your child. The ship begins to sink. You are the only one who can swim. You can save only one of the three. Who do you save?

This is a terrible dilemma, one in which you have to choose between three "goods". Almost everyone, regardless of cultural differences, would like to save all three. The critical issue is who do you choose, if you can only choose one. This is where cultural differences come in. Interestingly, in asking this question to more than 1,000 Asian and American managers in the course of cross-cultural training, we have discovered that Americans typically choose to save their child (approximately 65 percent of the time), with a smaller percentage choosing spouse and almost no one choosing mother. They explain their decision with such comments as, "My child has a future." "My child hasn't lived life yet." "My mother is old and has led her life." The majority of Asians over forty years of age most often will choose mother, justifying this choice by such comments as, "My mother is the one who took care of me. I owe her everything." "I can get another spouse or child, I can't get another mother." Asian managers under the age of forty, when asked the same question, responded more like the Americans, compared to the older Asians. This simple exercise points out a number of useful lessons about culture:

We act based upon our values

1)   Cultural values and beliefs form the core of our decision-making process. Generally, we act based upon our values — what we think and believe is important.

Different priorities mean different decisions

2)   Asians and Americans have many values in common. However, what is really important, when pushed to make a decision between competing values, is which is number one and which is number two. This is where culture becomes critically important, as Americans may make different decisions than Asians, based upon a different ordering of values.

Core values change over time

3)   Cultural values change over time. Asian societies have undergone tremendous changes over the last few decades. Their cultural values have also undergone changes. American society, as well, has gone through profound changes in the last few decades and some of the traditional values held by Americans are undergoing transition. Still, this change is relatively slow. The cultural values we received in our childhood tend to be firmly rooted. While we may be very flexible and adopt new ways of thinking and looking at the world when things are going well, our earliest and strongest values tend to reappear and reassert themselves when we are under pressure.

Generalizing about Culture

*Culture is
an important
part of
who we are*

It is obvious that everyone from the same culture doesn't think or act in the same way. This is because culture is just one (although a very significant one!) of the many influences that make up any individual. Each of us is influenced by at least three major factors: 1) biological or genetic factors which determine such things as physical size and emotional make up; 2) individual factors such as personality traits or life experiences which may dramatically affect who and what we are (i.e. going abroad for university study, growing up in poverty); and 3) the groups to which we belong. This third category is particularly interesting because, to some degree, we are affected by each and every group to which we belong. For example, let's take a look at Mr. Abdul Rahman, a Malay from Malaysia. We can define Mr. Rahman in terms of a mathematical formula:

$$Abdul\ Rahman = F(biological\ influences,\\ individual\ factors,\ group\ membership)$$

Mr. Rahman is married, has children, prays at the mosque every Friday, works as a petroleum engineer for a large American multinational company and plays on a football team after work. From this information, we know that Mr. Rahman belongs to the following groups: male, married, university-educated, Muslim, Malay, parent, engineer, soccer player. Each of these groups (and Mr. Rahman belongs to many others as well) to some degree or other, has influenced who Mr. Rahman is today. We can see that each of us, like Mr. Rahman, is a unique mix of biological influences, individual factors, and the influences of the groups to which we belong. While culture is only one of the groups to which each of us belongs, it is a very influential one and determines much of our behavior when we interact with other people. This explains why people from the same culture can be very different, yet at the same time show a number of important similarities.

Cultural generalizations are starting points for understanding others

What this means is that it is possible to make generalizations about people from different cultures. For example, we can comfortably state that, *in general*, Asian men are shorter than American men. However, we also know that there are some Asian men who are taller than the average American male and some American men who are shorter than the average Asian male.

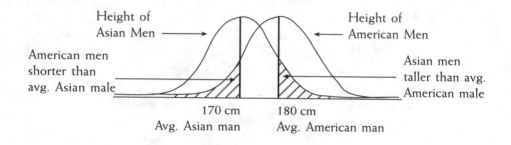

Height of Asian Men ⟶

Height of ⟵ American Men

American men shorter than avg. Asian male

Asian men taller than avg. American male

170 cm
Avg. Asian man

180 cm
Avg. American man

This type of generalizing seems obvious and we do it all the time. We know that in making generalizations there will be exceptions. It becomes less obvious when we make generalizations about cultural behavior. For example, we can safely say that *in general* Japanese save a larger portion of their income than Americans. Many studies have shown this to be true (Hall & Hall, 1987). However, we cannot say that *all* Japanese save more than *all* Americans because we can see that there are some Americans who are great savers and some Japanese who can't save at all.

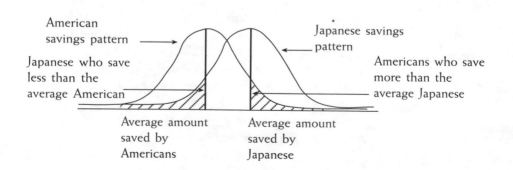

American savings pattern ⟶

Japanese savings pattern ⟵

Japanese who save less than the average American

Americans who save more than the average Japanese

Average amount saved by Americans

Average amount saved by Japanese

Limitations of generalizations

We can generalize about culture, and have to when working with people from other countries. Yet, we need to be very careful not to assume that everyone will fit the generalization. A generalization is only a working hypothesis, a starting place to help us understand those from a different culture.

The information that follows in this book is usually true for many, but not all, American managers. Each American manager is different, just as each Asian manager is different. However, it is possible to make some generalizations about values, beliefs and behaviors, recognizing that not every American will fit into the cultural mold.

The Culture Trap

Cultural near-sightedness

We all grow up learning our culture's ways of doing things. Other ways of doing things seem strange or funny — not quite right. It is easy to think of the way we do things in our own culture as the "right" or "normal" way — the way it should be. It often seems that the way people from other cultures do things is odd, peculiar, or just plain wrong. This is a natural tendency and one we all need to overcome in working for and with people who come from cultures very different from our own.

The citizens of any society which has been closed to the outside world or which traditionally has been able to meet most of its needs within its borders are even more likely to suffer from cultural nearsightedness than those who come from smaller countries which have a lot of contact with their neighbors. People from the U.S., China, Russia, Japan and India all deal with this issue. If you buy a world map made in America, chances are that the United States will be placed in the center of the map, thereby requiring Asia to be divided in half. To Americans, this makes sense because America is the center of their world. Not surprisingly, world maps made in China usually place China at the center.

Cultural near-sightedness, American-style

Notwithstanding the current interest of many businesspeople in the United States in Japanese management style, Pacific Rim economic development, and the dramatic globalization of businesses in the last few decades, many American managers remain quite narrow in their outlook. This is particularly true of those who have not travelled extensively or lived or worked overseas. Because of the United States' traditional history of isolation, of looking inward rather than outward, and because of the political and technological dominance of the U.S. in the last fifty years, many Americans believe that they can conduct business overseas from an American perspective. Because of this, they tend not to speak a foreign language well, have less interest in foreign affairs, and are less sophisticated in dealing in cross-cultural business situations than many of their trading partners.

Americans, in general, don't see themselves as holding "American" beliefs or values. They simply believe that the qualities and behaviors they see as important are those that matter to everyone. (Not surprisingly, Japanese, Chinese and many other Asians would believe the same thing.)

How Americans tend to view foreigners

Many Americans believe that the American way is the best, if not the only, way to do business. In part, this comes from America's history this century, of economic and political success. It also comes from America's past and present immigration experience, with people from all over the world wanting to settle in America. The logic goes something like this: "If so many people want to come to America, this must be the best place in the world." It is a very easy leap of thinking from that to believing that the American way of doing things must be the best. The result is that many Americans tend to expect that Asians and other non-Americans working with them will adapt to "the American Way".

The experience of most Americans has been that foreigners (non-Americans) are new immigrants, people on the way to becoming Americans, just like them. Foreigners in America are often treated as "odd" Americans, people who haven't quite (yet) learnt how to be American. This is quite different from what happens when an American lives in the Philippines, Thailand or Indonesia, or works for a Japanese or Korean company. In none of these cases would they be treated like an "odd" Thai, Japanese or Chinese, but rather as someone who comes from a different culture.

For the American in the home office dealing with an Asian manager 15,000 kilometers away, it is easy to expect that things will be done the American way. When an Asian manager takes a different approach to getting the job done, the American may feel confused or frustrated.

Asians through American eyes

Despite the attention the Pacific Rim has received in recent years, Americans, on the whole, are remarkably uninformed about Asia and Asian cultures. The majority of Americans have great difficulty distinguishing Koreans from Japanese or Japanese from Chinese. Many Americans cannot find where Singapore is on a world map. They cannot distinguish between Taiwan and Thailand. They are not sure if Indonesia is in Africa or Asia. For most of its history, America has looked to the countries of Europe as the focus of its attention. This is not surprising considering that these were the countries from which so many of America's founders and early immigrants came. Americans have traditionally viewed Europe and America as more important and the other nations of the world as somewhat less important.

There is a common misconception which occurs when Americans travel to Asia. They see the skyscrapers of Asian cities, the high tech offices and the sophisticated staff and often they assume that Asia has become Westernized. The reality is that Asia has become modern, not Western, in the last few decades. You need to help your American colleagues see the difference.

Traditional stereotypes of Asians

What the average American knows about Asia historically came from his or her exposure to movies about Asia or Asians, America's Asian immigrant history, and three major wars fought in Asia this century. The traditional image or stereotype, which only now is changing, lumped all Asians together in a picture that was neither attractive nor accurate. These stereotypes were based on limited person-to-person contact and misinformation or partial information about Asian cultures. They were the result of cultural nearsightedness and the filtering of information through American cultural glasses.

On the positive side of this generalization of Asians,

people from Pacific Rim countries were seen as hard workers, family-oriented, ambitious, smart and interested in getting a good education. On the negative side, they were seen as clannish (only stayed with their own people) and lacking in feelings (Americans called them "inscrutable" because their cultural glasses made it hard for Americans to read Asian expressions of emotion). They were thought of as sly or sneaky because of things like the surprise attack on Pearl Harbor in World War II or guerrilla warfare in Vietnam. It traditionally has been hard for Americans to "figure out" Asians.

Americans'
concerns
about Asia
and Asians

In the last decade or so, another picture is emerging. The economic news filling American newspapers almost daily tells the story of the increasing economic power and competitiveness of Asian business. There is a concern that Asians will not only outpace Americans, but will also displace them. American jobs going abroad and Asians buying land and businesses in the U.S. are a significant concern for the average American.

The net result today is that many Americans start out with both positive and negative attitudes towards Asians. Many Asian values and behaviors are ones they admire and respect. Other values and behaviors are ones they have a great difficulty understanding and appreciating. Still others, are ones they can neither figure out nor see as making sense.

A Strategy for Cross-Cultural Effectiveness: Being a "Winner" at Work

To be successful in working with American managers, you need to develop and be comfortable in using four major sets of skills:

1)   The ability to see differences as "just different", rather than as "bad" or "good".
2)   An understanding of how American managers generally think and act on the job.
3)   An ability and willingness to switch your working style when it will increase your effectiveness.
4)   The ability and willingness to serve as a cross-cultural guide to the Americans whom you work with.

Letting go of "good" and "bad"

A critical skill for anyone working cross-culturally is the ability to see different ways of doing things as just that — different, rather than as "good" or "bad". As should be clear by now, it is not unusual when introduced to another culture, to be struck by many differences in the way people do things — everything from eating (chop sticks vs. hands vs. knife and fork) to driving, to how one treats a guest (especially when the guest is you!). You know your own culture's rules for how to handle each of these situations. When you come across a different approach, it is easy to judge that approach as bad or wrong, especially when it is so different to what you are used to that it seems rude or offensive to you. In business, it quickly becomes very clear that there are different cultural rules on how to disagree politely, the role of the boss/subordinate, how decisions get made, plus many more.

In these situations it is easy to be critical and to judge these differences as bad. It is much more useful, however, to try to see differences as just different — arising out of cultural rules and glasses which are unlike your own. In most cases, these differences are not intended to cause frustration, embarrassment or discomfort. They are merely the "way things are done" by those from a different culture. You don't have to adopt these practices or even like them. Yet, if you can keep a neutral attitude towards them, recognizing that they are cultural traits a person brings to the workplace rather than individual traits designed to frustrate and confuse you, you will have an easier time working with people from another culture.

Learning what to expect from American managers

Being successful cross-culturally requires that you understand where the basic points of difference are between those of your culture and those of the other culture with regard to your ways of thinking and doing things at work. Generally, you will find that there are areas where you think, act and react quite similarly. You will also find areas where your thoughts, actions and reactions are very different. To the degree that you can understand and anticipate these differences, you can work to bridge the gap between your ways and American ways.

To make this clearer, let's consider the area of personal questions. Usually what Americans define as too personal to talk about with colleagues from work is different from what most Asians would consider too personal. For example, many Asians are not uncomfortable discussing their salaries and benefits with their colleagues. In many Asian offices, there are no secrets about such things. These kind of questions would seem too personal for most Americans. Knowing this, you can avoid asking a question which would embarrass your American colleague. Since you are both interested in maintaining a good working relationship, this kind of information can be very useful to you. Knowing such things as the American style of decision-making, maintaining good working relationships or negotiating, can provide you with valuable insights into how to be a "winner" with your American counterpart and, at the same time, experience less frustration yourself at work.

Learning about mainstream American business culture

Even though management styles are undergoing change in American society, much of what has been traditional remains. Cultural change, as stated previously, is a very slow process. The cultural influences and perspectives that have historically steered American management still exist. They remain the core of American business today. In a July, 1990 *Wall Street Journal* survey, more than two-thirds of management staff positions of both large and small American companies were held by white males. Twenty-three percent were held by white women. Likewise, ninety-five percent of American managers posted overseas were male (Fernandez, 1993). Traditional European-American culture has been the mainstream business culture in the United States and has dictated the standards to which Americans from other cultural backgrounds have been, and continue to be, expected to conform. This is particularly true in large multinational companies which have offices and staff abroad. For this reason, it is the culture of the white middle class American male manager that is reflected in this book. It is their values and behavior that have shaped American business. (For a discussion of the impact and implications of increasing diversity in American management, see Chapter 3, "The Changing American Workplace".)

Switching styles — using what works

When you are with your boss, you act in a certain way, a way that is suited to your boss. When you leave the office and visit your mother, you act in yet another way, switching to a style more suited to her. Those of you with children know that when you talk with them, you switch your style yet again. In each case, you are adjusting your approach, switching your style, so as to be more effective. This same skill can be very valuable to you in a cross-cultural work setting. If you work for an American multinational company or if your boss is an American, you can increase your effectiveness by consciously choosing to style-switch in certain situations. By changing your approach from the one you generally use to one more familiar to the Americans with whom you work, you can improve the likelihood that communication will be enhanced and that the job will be accomplished more smoothly and easily.

In the course of your education and work experience you have developed a working style, a way of relating to others on the job, of approaching the tasks at hand, of dealing with the world of work. If you have been successful, your style probably has served you well. It allows you to get the job done in your own culture. What style-switching means is that there are other approaches to these same ends, approaches which you can choose to adopt when it suits your purposes. You don't change as a person, you just become more effective.

Cross-cultural understanding goes two ways

Of course, what we're talking about here is not a one-way process. Americans need to follow exactly the same strategies for cross-cultural effectiveness in learning how to work with Asian bosses, colleagues and subordinates. While much of the management literature and many of the management theories have come out of the United States in the last few decades, the American way is not the "right" or only way to work with and manage people effectively. There are many paths to the same end. The American model of management is just one.

Becoming a cross-cultural guide

Just as you can increase your effectiveness by increasing your understanding of American cultural rules and glasses, you can help the Americans with whom you work to gain the same kind of understanding about your culture. You can serve as a guide to your culture. Helping Americans develop an appreciation of the rules and glasses of your culture will make it easier for you to work together. The American manager, whether based in Asia or the United States, can benefit from the cross-cultural understanding which your perspective can bring.

Facing the challenge for today's global manager

If you work for an American company abroad, the real challenge is to combine the values and management styles of your own culture with that of American culture and your company's corporate culture. For Americans, their challenge is exactly the same. They must take into account the rules and glasses of your culture, their own background, and the corporate culture and expectations of the company.

This book will encourage you to see differences among work colleagues as just different rather than good or bad and to practice style-switching when and where appropriate. It will offer you an overview of how American managers generally think, communicate, and operate on the job. It will provide you with suggestions on how to be a cross-cultural guide. We believe that with this preparation, you will be able to become a more effective cross-cultural manager, increasingly able to deal with a wide range of colleagues in today's global business environment.

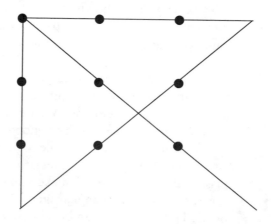

Solution to puzzle on page 7.

2
The Origins of Asian and American Cultures

Culture
makes
sense

Culture makes sense. It is a logical and rational response to specific environmental, historical or geographic conditions. It is society's attempt to deal with the world around it in order to maximize the chances for survival and minimize conflict between people.

For example, let's look at the Chinese cultural definition of food. What can and cannot be eaten is defined very broadly in Chinese culture. In fact, almost anything that breathes or grows has a place on the Chinese table. This makes sense given China's long history of famine. By widely defining what is and what is not food, Chinese culture put all that was available to the greatest use. This increased the chances of survival for the greatest number of people.

Of course, no one individual consciously made this decision for an entire society, but the culture evolved over hundreds of years in directions that were best for survival at that time. This was accomplished in a very interesting way. Those food items which would not immediately and easily be seen as food (i.e. sea slugs, fish heads) were elevated to the status of delicacies, making them high status foods. This made it easier for them to be accepted by the general population. The stranger the food, the more of a delicacy it became.

While specific cultural rules and glasses make sense at one time in a society's history, changes such as economic development, urbanization, technology, and education can make a culture's responses outdated. Very few Chinese in Taiwan, Hong Kong or in China suffer from the fear of starvation today. Yet, traditional cultural concepts of what food is persist. Cultures change slower than the reality which surrounds them.

In America, the custom of carrying a gun to defend yourself made sense when each man had to defend himself and his family living on the frontier. Today, that same frontier has been settled. Yet, Americans are killing each other with guns in record numbers. Somehow, the cultural belief that each American should be able to carry a weapon persists. This makes no sense to many visitors to the U.S. (nor to many Americans!). Yet it carries the weight of a strong cultural tradition and will only change slowly and with great effort.

Culture changes more slowly than reality

What this means is that the rules and glasses of a culture often lag behind current day realities. They are attempts to adjust to a particular set of conditions that may not exist today. Although these rules and glasses may be outdated, they still are accepted and practiced by the vast majority. Therefore, to really make sense out of any culture, we need to understand the particular historical, economic or political environment in which it evolved. If we can see how it once made sense, then it will be easier to understand the people of that culture today.

Origins of Asian cultural values

The countries of Asia have their own unique religious, geographical and historical backgrounds which make each of them different from its neighbors. Islam in Malaysia and Indonesia, Buddhism in Thailand, Christianity in the Philippines, Japan's isolation from the rest of the world, China's Confucian philosophy, have all led to very different cultures and approaches to the world. While there is great diversity among the cultures of East and Southeast Asia today, there are some common factors that are shared by most Asians.

Asian cultures evolved out of conditions in which the majority of the people were rural farmers. They lived in small villages, barely surviving from year to year. If you were born in a village, you were likely to die there. The village was crowded and there was limited new land to develop. You lived with, and were dependent upon, your extended family — parents, aunts, uncles, cousins. Keeping social peace and harmony was critical. Life was dangerous, with the threat of wars, diseases, famines, and natural disasters, such as floods and typhoons, being regular occurrences. Life was very hard. Society's goal was survival — allowing people to get by day-by-day. These common conditions, shared by many Asian societies, form the environment out of which many Asian cultures developed. It was in these small, poor villages, with limited mobility and emphasis upon survival, that many of the values, assumptions, patterns of thinking and communication of many Asian people today had their beginnings. Even so, it is important to note that Southeast Asian cultures evolved out of environments that were less harsh than those of East Asia. Concern about survival, therefore, was not as crucial on a daily basis for people who came from environments with less harsh weather conditions and less population pressure. This, in part, explains some of the significant differences between East and Southeast Asian cultures. Another difference is the shared tradition of Confucian customs and beliefs common in most East Asian cultures.

Origins of American cultural values

American culture evolved over the last few hundred years out of a very different set of circumstances. Understanding these conditions helps one understand why Americans act as they do today. The first Americans, called Native-Americans (Indians) came originally, over many centuries, from northern Asia. They were few in number and lived in scattered settlements throughout what is now the United States and Canada. The second wave of immigrants came from Europe. These people were of two types: 1) those who disagreed with the politics or religion of their former home and were looking for religious or political freedom; and/or, 2) those who were looking for economic opportunities in a new land. They were the risk-takers, willing or forced to make major changes in hopes of a better life. They came one-by-one or family-by-family, cut off from the support of their extended families back home. They left the social hierarchies of Europe behind. They believed each person could make a place for himself or herself based on hard work and effort. They brought with them European traditions which placed great emphasis on rational thinking, Christian beliefs, and following society's and God's laws. (There were also a large number of Africans in these early years who came as slaves, against their will, who also played a role in America's newly developing culture.)

They found a land underpopulated, resource-rich, and theirs for the taking. (Although Native Americans lived in much of America for centuries before the arrival of the Europeans, they lacked the resources to defend their land from a technologically superior opponent.) With hard work and the abundant resources they found, they were able to thrive and prosper. They viewed this new world as essentially boundless, with land and opportunities stretching westward as far as they could imagine. They viewed themselves as independent, in control of their own destinies, and proud of what their hard work had accomplished. Out of these early experiences in American history came the values of respect for individual freedom, a belief in equality and democracy, skepticism towards tradition and authority, and boundless optimism for the future.

The frontier experience

American culture developed along two major themes. One was the myth and reality of the Frontier. This is the story of the pioneers who settled the West. In the 1800s, as population growth put pressure on available farmland on the eastern coast, Americans moved westward. Individuals and families, often just a husband and wife with their children, left the relatively comfortable, settled life of extended family and friends. They ventured to remote areas to farm, ranch and prospect for gold. Once again, people left what was known and journeyed to the unknown in search of a better life. They could take that risk because land was free and economic opportunities, abundant. These people lived difficult, lonely lives, isolated from others. They were responsible for their own success or failure. They had only themselves or their immediate families on which to rely.

Many of America's legends and folk stories are based on the lives of these people and their adventures. These pioneers are glorified in American folk history, as adventurers who overcame insurmountable odds to "conquer the West". They came to be viewed, whether accurately or not, as models of the American ideal, how Americans like to view themselves. Many of the values of American culture today, such as independence, individualism, hard work, risk-taking and self-reliance, came directly from the pioneer experience on the American Frontier.

Industrializa-
tion promotes
value of
control

Another major theme in American culture, that of man's ability to control his environment, arose out of the industrial revolution which started in Europe. Americans quickly developed cities that were centers of industry and technology. They built bridges, dams and railroads across the country. Americans proudly talk about "taming the continent". Factories brought people into the cities where great wealth was produced. People learned to work and live with others who were not from their village or family, people with whom they had little or no personal relationship. They became mobile and saw that change and development brought greater prosperity for all. This experience convinced Americans that, with proper planning and effort, almost anything can be accomplished. It reinforced the message that individuals are able to affect social and economic change. For Americans, and especially Americans in business, control (of their world, of their business, of their lives) became a critical social value and one that forms the core of a lot of business decisions today.

Roots of Asian and American Cultures

Asian	American
1. Family or small group as basic unit of society	1. Individual as basic unit of society
2. Emphasis on survival	2. Emphasis on control
3. Life was dangerous/ hard	3. Life presented opportunities
4. Rural/ agricultural	4. Urban/Industrial as well as rural
5. Limited economic opportunities	5. Expanding economic opportunities
6. Slow or no change	6. Rapid change
7. Crowded	7. Underpopulated

Control and individualism became keynotes of the American character while practicality, survival orientation, and concern about the group formed the basic values of many Asian societies. As we will see, these very different environments, and the values that arose from them, caused American and Asian cultures to develop in very different ways.

3
The Changing American Workplace

America traditionally has been referred to as a "melting pot," where people of many races, cultures, and religions came together to find opportunity. That term was appropriate when the majority of immigrants were from Northern Europe. Today, America is more accurately described as a "salad bowl" in which people from different backgrounds and orientations mix and interact with each other, but also maintain their cultural or racial identity.

Americans come in many colors and speak many languages. African-Americans (blacks), Hispanics (Spanish-speaking Americans) and Asian-Americans make up more than 24 percent of the American population. This diversity is increasing, with growing immigration from Latin America and Asia. Between 1980 and 1990, the African-American population increased by 13 percent, the Hispanic population, by 53 percent, and the Asian-American population, by an incredible 108 percent. During this same time, the white American population grew by only 6 percent (U.S. Department of Commerce, 1992). Many predict that sometime in the next century whites who trace their ancestry to Europe will become the minority in America.

The changing workforce

Today, one out of every three new workers is a non-white minority person. In 1990, 11 percent of the work force was black, while 8 percent was Hispanic. The fastest growing portion of the American workforce is Asian-American (U.S. Department of Commerce, 1992). By the year 2000, minorities will account for more than one quarter of the total work force.

Presently, women account for a little less than half the work force. Almost three-quarters of women between the ages of twenty and forty-four work in America, a considerable increase from past decades. Two out of every three new American jobs today are filled by women (Fernandez, 1993).

Changing management

As the American workforce changes, the picture of American management is changing as well. In the past, American management was staffed almost entirely by white males. This is no longer true today and will be even less true in the future. Women, African-Americans, Hispanic-Americans, and others previously excluded from the ranks of middle and upper management, are beginning to take their place. In the last five years, there has been a 36 percent increase in minorities in management in American corporations and a 68 percent increase in women (Nelton, 1992). These new managers bring with them different perspectives and orientations, different cultural rules and glasses.

American Women at Work

*American
women
managers*

More and more women are assuming positions in American management. In 1972, 19 percent of management positions in business were held by women; by the end of 1990, that figure more than doubled to 40 percent (Fernandez, 1993). While this growth has primarily been at the lower and middle levels of management, it reflects a great change in the way of thinking and is an indication of trends to come.

*Women
managers
expect equal
treatment*

Traditionally, there were clear and distinct ideas about appropriate ways to treat men and women in American society. Now, the rules are changing. The distinction between male and female roles at work, particularly in management positions, is quickly disappearing in the U.S. An American woman manager often views herself as a manager first and a woman second, when she is in the workplace. This means she expects to be treated no differently than her male colleagues in terms of promotional opportunities, salary, or responsibilities assigned to her. Equal treatment is the law in the United States and many women have overcome significant obstacles to get to the positions they now hold. There is great sensitivity with regard to this issue because of inequalities and discrimination in the past. The Asian manager working with American women executives is well served by understanding and respecting the tremendous changes that have and are occurring around this issue in American business today.

*Sexual
harassment*

Recent court cases have made American management extremely sensitive to issues of sexual discrimination and harassment. Comments or gestures which are objectionable or cause discomfort or humiliation are no longer permitted in American business. This includes sexual jokes, comments about someone's body, unwanted touching, and unwelcome sexual advances. This can be a confusing issue for the Asian manager. It may be hard to judge where the line is between just being friendly and being sexually inappropriate.

> **What This Means For You:**
>
> *To prevent yourself from getting into trouble, follow these simple rules when interacting with American women in the workplace:*
> 1. *Don't assume that friendliness on the part of your American colleague means sexual interest;*
> 2. *If you get any signs, verbal or non-verbal, that a behavior of yours is not welcome or appropriate, stop the behavior immediately;*
> 3. *If you are not sure whether a behavior or comment is appropriate or not, don't do or say it. Ask an American colleague what's the right thing to do or say in that situation.*

Minorities in the Workplace

Minorities play an increasing role in American management

America is a society of many cultures. Minority groups form important sub-cultures in American society. As women have begun to advance into the ranks of management in America, so have business professionals from minority groups. Although they are still underrepresented in management compared to their percentage in the American population at large, their numbers are growing. In 1991, African-Americans and Hispanics represented 6.3 percent and 3.7 percent respectively of those employed in management and professional specialties. This was a growth of 13 percent for African-Americans and 42 percent for Hispanics from just eight years earlier (U.S. Department of Commerce, 1992). As their numbers increase and as they continue to assume greater leadership roles in American business, the traditional rules and glasses of American business that came from the Northern European white societies are bound to change.

If you are working with numbers of Americans, you will inevitably come into contact with African-Americans, Hispanics, Asian-Americans and, perhaps, Native Americans (Indians). As with women, equal treatment is expected and required under U.S. law.

What This Means For You:

Do not treat minorities any differently from other Americans. Avoid comments stating or implying racial or ethnic minorities are not as capable, intelligent or efficient as either Asians or other Americans.

African-
Americans

Black Americans are the largest minority group in the United States. In 1990, thirty million African-Americans made up 12 percent of the American population (U.S. Department of Commerce, 1992). Distinct from all the other sub-cultures in America, they carry with them the unique history of slavery. They were the only group that did not come to America out of their own choice. Because of this and the legacy of prejudice and racism that exists in the U.S., they, as a group, have had great difficulties becoming full participants in American society. Older African-American adults can remember times in certain parts of the United States where black people could not go to white schools, eat in white restaurants or sit in the front of public buses. In many parts of the country, blacks still confront racial prejudice.

Many African-Americans are well-educated and many have entered the ranks of the middle class. Nonetheless, there remains a significant proportion who are trapped in poverty and unemployment. African-Americans, more than any other group in the U.S., live in two worlds. Like white Americans, they are a part of the larger American culture. At the same time, they have a strong sense of feeling separate from it.

Hispanics

Hispanics are the second largest minority group in the United States. In 1990, they were 9 percent of the total population of the U.S.A. or more than twenty-two million Americans (U.S. Department of Commerce, 1992). They are from many Spanish-speaking countries, each with its own culture, history, and racial make-up. People who originally came from Mexico, Puerto Rico, and Cuba form the three largest sub-groups. In some parts of the United States (the Southwest, southern Florida), Hispanics form the majority of the population.

Some Hispanics can trace their roots in the United States back for centuries. Others have arrived more recently to escape political turmoil or to better themselves economically. While many Hispanics are well-educated, successful, and have entered the ranks of the American middle class, on the whole, the living standard of Hispanics in the United States is lower than that of the average American. This occurs, in part, because of the large numbers of illegal immigrants in this group. Their lack of legal status and low levels of education keep them in low-paying jobs. With the growth of this population in the U.S.A. and with increasing interest in Latin American markets, Hispanics inevitably will play a larger role in management in American companies.

Asian-Americans

Asian-Americans are the fastest growing minority group in America. More than seven million Asians and Pacific Islanders were recorded in the 1990 census (U.S. Department of Commerce, 1992). The three largest Asian sub-populations are Chinese, Filipinos, and Japanese. There are significant numbers of Vietnamese, Thais, and Koreans as well. They live throughout America, but are concentrated in California, Hawaii, and the Washington, D.C. area.

In the last few decades, many Asian-Americans have been remarkably successful in integrating into the larger American society. They have been viewed as a "model minority," with household incomes higher than that of the average white American family (Fernandez, 1993). This has been accomplished, in part, because of their smaller numbers, educational achievements, and cultural values of hard work and thrift.

In recent years, with a massive influx of Asian immigrants, many of whom were uneducated and unskilled, some problems have begun to emerge and anti-Asian attitudes have begun to appear. As concern about Asian economic success, both in Asia and at home, has grown, instances of tension and even violence have also increased.

Asian-Americans in Asia

More and more American multinational companies with offices in Asia are sending Asian-Americans to Asia in management positions. This makes sense. Not only are these managers, in many cases, fluent in the local language, they often are familiar with the culture and ways of doing business. These individuals tend to be immigrants who have maintained close ties to the language and culture of their homelands. However, it is important for the Asian manager to recognize that other Asian-Americans posted to Asia, who were born and raised in America, may not speak any Asian language or be familiar with Asian cultural traditions. They may have Asian faces, but look at the world through American cultural glasses and follow American cultural rules.

The challenge of diversity

In order to work effectively with American managers today, you need to understand the traditional American cultural rules and glasses of managers, such as those presented in this book. Additionally, you will need to factor in the different rules and glasses which women and minorities may bring to the work place. On top of that, you must take individual differences into account. This is the challenge which the diversity of the American workforce presents.

4
American Patterns of Thinking

Mr. Hernandez, the new American CEO of an American subsidiary in Bangkok, decided to have a "brainstorming" session in which all were encouraged to shout ideas as they occurred to them. The session was based on the assumption that although most of these spontaneous ideas wouldn't be useful, the technique might open communications and lead to creative thinking. Perhaps one idea that emerged could be developed and refined. Khun Jadung, a senior Thai manager, watched in amazement, certain that his fellow Thai managers would not allow themselves to offer unexamined ideas and possibly appear foolish. His boss, on the other hand, wondered why Khun Jadung and the other managers had so little to contribute and why they seemed unwilling to get into the spirit of the session.

Culture determines how you think

The way we think, that is, the way we mentally process information, seems natural and normal to us. It is difficult to imagine that there may be other ways of thinking. In reality, the way we think is very dependent upon our culture. People who come from different cultures can, and often do, have dramatically different ways of thinking, of mentally making sense out of the information they receive.

Thinking develops like a muscle

One way of looking at this issue is to imagine that the way you develop your method of thinking is like the way you develop certain muscles in your body. If you jogged five kilometers every day for a year, the muscles in your calves and thighs would certainly get stronger and larger. Alternatively, if you did fifty push-ups every day for a year, your chest and arms would be developed. Patterns of thinking develop like muscles do in that the processes you use on a regular basis become stronger. Those you don't use become weaker and you are less able to use them. Patterns of thinking are not determined by biology or genetics, but by what you practice, and that pattern of practice is determined by your culture.

Asian educational systems

One way to see this clearly is to look at the educational systems of most Asian countries. Although some of these systems are currently undergoing change, most Asian managers over the age of 25 received their basic education from systems that had their roots in traditional cultures. (One exception here may be the Philippines where the style of education has been patterned on the American model.)

In a traditional Asian educational system, the goal of education is to transmit the wisdom of the past. Continuity is emphasized. The role of the student is to accept these learnings as presented in traditional writings and books as well as by the teacher. The student is expected to work hard, not to question, and to be able to repeat back the knowledge she or he has learned. As in Japanese or Chinese calligraphy, there is only one right way to do something; nothing else is allowed. The process is basically one-way. The teacher presents the information and the student passively receives it. The classroom is disciplined and orderly. Asking questions is seen as a challenge to the teacher's authority or as an admission of your own ignorance. Neither is desirable.

In Asian countries which have languages derived from idiographic or picture characters, students must spend thousands of hours mastering the basic 3-5,000 characters needed just to read a newspaper. In Taiwan, Hong Kong, and China, for example, you see students spending countless hours memorizing and practicing in their copy books how to write those thousands of characters. Similarly, it is estimated that high school graduates in Japan are expected to know at least 2,000 *kanji* characters.

Asians learn to be good at memorizing, concentrating, and focusing on details

Students who have gone through a traditional Asian education become very good at what they have practiced for thousands of hours. As adults, their patterns of thinking, their "thinking muscles" are well developed for being able to memorize and to retain large amounts of information. Their learning has required discipline. Skills in concentrating, working hard and persistently at a task, not complaining, paying attention to fine detail, and accepting and respecting the wisdom of authority figures are all developed through their educational experience. Education is practical, providing the reading, writing and mathematical skills students need to succeed in the world. These are the patterns of thinking in which most Asians have been trained. Therefore, they are the patterns of thinking with which most Asians are comfortable.

American educational system

Typically, American students have a very different experience in their initial years of formal education. When American parents are asked what they want their child to gain from school, they often say something like, "I want my child to be able to think for herself." Or, "I want my child to learn to make good decisions, to stand up for what he believes in and to be able to deal effectively with the challenges of modern day living." When an American youngster goes to school, she only has to memorize 26 "characters" — A, B, C, D, etc., to be a literate person. She then learns to put them together in different ways to form words. The process is one of combining old knowledge to create something new.

In class, the teacher encourages students to discuss and debate issues, to learn how to solve problems, and often to create their own answers to questions posed. Americans prefer learning through personal discovery and problem-solving rather than memorizing facts presented to them by an authority figure. Ideally, the emphasis is on learning how to think independently, how to analyze logically, and how to problem-solve creatively. The teacher views questions from students as learning opportunities, rather than as challenges to her authority. The ideal American classroom is a seemingly chaotic environment, with lots of different activities going on and children learning independently and at their own pace. Discussion, debate, and questions are common. The teacher's job is to promote creativity, individual initiative, and responsibility. The role is often as much that of a catalyst, to get students to think, as that of a conveyor of knowledge.

What This Means For You:

If an American asks a question, it is probably not a challenge to your authority or knowledge, but rather an attempt to gain information. When you don't understand something or need more information, the American expects you will ask a question.

Americans learn to be good at analyzing, creating, and debating

The net result, after 12 or more years of such education, is that the patterns of thinking, the "thinking muscles," of the typical American are very different from those of the Asian colleague. The successful results of American education are adults who are good at, and comfortable with, analyzing problems, being creative, debating and disagreeing with colleagues, and combining information to arrive at a new solution. They become competent in estimating the possibilities for success or failure in any given course of action, strong in weighing options and risks.

How Americans problem-solve

Most American managers are at ease dealing with the theoretical and philosophical. They have been encouraged to ask "Why?" and have been rewarded for coming up with their own answers. However, they are most comfortable thinking from the small to the large, from the specific to the general. When Americans think of a project, task or problem, they generally break it down into its component parts and build from the ground up.

The importance of facts

Facts are important to Americans. They have been taught to believe that there is information, independent of any individual, that can be researched and found that supports an argument or makes a case. Using facts is generally considered the best way to make a point. Facts make opinions valid, accurate or truthful. Many Asians are surprised at the amount of facts, and especially the amount of numbers and statistics, American managers use in their daily conversations. For example, an Asian manager might say, "She's out of the country for a short time." His American colleague is likely to say, "This is a short trip. She'll be away for six days. She makes this trip three or four times a year. Forty percent of her time . . ."

What This Means For You:

When presenting an idea or plan to an American manager, justify it by presenting facts and figures that support your position. When American managers make decisions, they want to do it on the basis of "hard data", not opinions or personal feelings.

American logic

Americans tend to believe that most events have a discoverable cause. Things don't just happen, but are caused by something. They try to express their ideas showing clear cause and effect. This means the line of reasoning is linear and logical (like a ruler or tape measure, A follows B and leads to C) and is supported by observable facts or data. On the whole, facts and logic are more highly valued than intuition in business. Americans usually are uncomfortable with thinking which they describe as "fuzzy" — not focused on the task, rambling, or which brings in points not directly relevant to the issue at hand.

Different comfort zones

An American professor who teaches both Asian and American students summed up the different patterns of thinking in this way: "I tell my American students that it's not enough to be able to think. You have to have something in your head to think about. I need to give Asian students just the opposite advice. The problem isn't that Asian students don't have enough in their heads to think about. They have memorized tremendous amounts of information. It is the problem of being creative, thinking things through freshly," (Durrant, 1989). If you ask most Americans to memorize and retain a large amount of information, you will generally find they are uncomfortable with the task. The thinking muscles, or patterns of thinking required, just aren't highly developed in this area for most Americans. It's not that Americans can't memorize, but rather that their experience doesn't prepare them well for such a task. It is out of their comfort zone. Similarly, if you ask Asians, who have had a traditional education with limited exposure to Western business practices, to participate in brainstorming sessions, they often feel uncomfortable and perhaps not very confident. It is out of their comfort zone.

What This Means For You:

If you are uncomfortable in a problem-solving or brainstorming session, or when asked to state your opinion in front of a group, recognize that this behavior may be out of your comfort zone. You can build your skills in these areas through practice. Work to develop your "thinking muscles" in areas that directly affect your job performance.

When people who have different ways of reasoning or thinking interact and work with each other, it is easy for either one or both of them to believe that the other isn't being logical or clear or that the other just isn't making sense. It is easy to be misunderstood. Both Asian and American managers need to pay particular attention to how they organize and express their thoughts and arguments when speaking and writing. Unless they do, they will have difficulty being understood by colleagues from a different culture.

Section II: Relationships on the Job

5
The Individualistic American

Cultures in Contrast: Individualism vs. Concern for the Group

A group of American teachers were invited to attend National Day ceremonies in Taipei. They were each given an official badge to wear for entry into the restricted visitors' area. Unlike their Chinese counterparts, who all consciously placed the badges on the same place on the lapels of their suit jackets, the Americans consciously placed the badges on different parts of their suits and on the front of their pants. Some just slipped the badges into their pockets. They did not intend to give offense or to show disrespect. They were just asserting their unique individuality and resisting the pressure to be "just like everyone else".

Asian cultures are group-based

The group is the basic unit of society in Asian cultures. This means that individuals in an Asian society are defined, to a great extent, by the groups to which they belong. They are a kind of intersection of roles which they play in various groups. This emphasis upon the group and de-emphasis of the individual can be seen, for example, in the Asian reaction to the following comment, "I really admire you because you are the type of person who does precisely what you think is right, no matter what others may think." Most Americans would take this as a compliment, considering it a good thing to fulfill your individuality, to do what you want to do, without being overly concerned about the opinions of others. Most Asians would not see this as a compliment at all, and instead, might think, "What do you mean I don't care what others think about me! I have to be concerned about how others see me."

Group-based cultures make survival more likely

A group-based culture made sense for many traditional Asian civilizations. In poor, crowded, agricultural societies, people had to cooperate to survive. In times when people were living on the edge, when one natural or man-made difficulty could mean a disaster, the small group — the family, the village, or the clan — working together, helped to make sure that life would go on.

Attention to relationships is important in group-based cultures

To ensure cooperation, keeping relationships functioning smoothly was very important. If there were problems between people in the family, between neighbors, or in the village, all would suffer. Maintaining harmony and smooth relations with the people you had to deal with on a daily basis was critical to survival. Even today, when survival is no longer the primary concern, everyone in a group-based culture continues to be concerned about the harmony of the group as a whole, as well as among members of the group. While beneath the surface in an Asian family, younger sister may not get along with elder brother, or middle brother may disagree with father's decisions, it is important, on the surface, to maintain a degree of harmony, to ensure that differences and disagreements do not boil over and destroy the smooth functioning of the group. To do this, Asian cultures have encouraged people to pay attention to relationships. From a very early age, Asians learn ways to ensure smooth relationships — ways to "give people face" (maintain dignity and respect) and ways to prevent people from "losing face". In Asian societies, today as well as in the past, much time and energy is spent keeping important relationships in good order.

In many Asian countries, a famous American fast food restaurant recognizes its outstanding performers by posting, where all employees and patrons can see, a picture of "The Crew of the Month". This same company in America follows the same method of employee recognition, with just one difference. In the U.S., it is the "Employee of the Month". The individual, rather than the group, is honored.

American culture is individualistic

The individual is the basic unit of society in American culture. If you listen to a discussion between two Americans, you will hear the word "I" used many times more than you will hear "we". In Asia, it is the reverse. When introducing himself, a Japanese businessman will often state the name of his company before his own name; an American businessman almost always will introduce himself first. The first question an American asks is, "What do you do?" The first question a Japanese asks is, "What company do you work for?"

In America, great emphasis is placed on the individual being and achieving all he or she can. Americans sing songs proclaiming, "I've got to be me," (follow your own desires). They voice slogans like, "Do your own thing," (do what you want, not what others want you to do). "Look out for number one," (take care of yourself first). Americans believe that it is important for them to "be themselves". They see less reason to adjust their behavior from one social situation to another than do their Asian counterparts.

Signs of individualism can be seen everywhere in American society in small and large ways. When you meet Americans for the first time, they will likely ask you to call them by their first names, rather than by their family names. Their identity is as individuals, first and foremost, and only secondarily as members of a family or group. When American friends go out for lunch, they often divide the bill, each paying his or her own share. You will hear Americans saying things like, "If you want something done right, you've got to do it by yourself," or "In the long run, the only person you can count on is yourself."

Roots of American individualism

As discussed previously, the American emphasis on the individual grew out of the country's frontier experience and its history as a land of immigrants. Traditionally, the United States has been a place where a person would come with little or nothing and carve out a life for him or herself. Often separated by thousands of miles from family and friends, individuals had only themselves and their immediate families to depend upon for survival.

Americans see themselves as unique

Americans like to think of themselves as unique, not as following the rules or expectations of the group, even though, in reality, most of them are remarkably similar to their fellow Americans. It is the value which is important, even though it may not always be followed. American heroes are individuals who have achieved great things on their own, often against great odds. The classic American action movie tells the story of the individual who is a rebel, who doesn't quite fit in. He's the detective who ignores the rules of the police department to solve the case by himself. He's the lone cowboy who rides into town and, single-handedly, defeats the "bad guys". The American hero solves the problem his own way, triumphing against the forces of evil, often represented by a group.

To achieve success through your own efforts has been a theme from the Frontier days to the present. Americans typically want to be their own boss, to have the freedom and independence to make their own decisions. No praise can be higher than to say to an American, "You are your own person," meaning, you alone decide what is right for you.

Americans resist generalizations about themselves

Interestingly, because of this emphasis on personal uniqueness, Americans resist generalizations made about American culture. While Japanese (or Filipinos or Chinese or Vietnamese) might say, "We Japanese act . . . .," it is far less common to hear an American say, "We Americans believe . . . . " Many Americans feel that to be grouped together as one culture is an insult to their uniqueness as individuals. They are uncomfortable with the fact that their behavior may be culturally-based and, therefore, predictable. It goes against the value of individuality.

The importance of freedom

Because of the value Americans place on individualism, individual freedom is also a very powerful idea in American culture. Freedom to make choices, freedom to behave as you wish as long as you don't harm others, freedom to believe what you want, are all of great importance to Americans. Americans dislike being told what to do. When asked in a survey, "What are you proudest of about America?", 71 percent responded with "Freedom" or "Liberty" (Civic Service, 1981).

There is a great emphasis on protecting the rights of the individual in American society, sometimes at the expense of the common good. The right to sue in court, to speak your mind in public, to sit in a smoke-free environment, to attend the religious institution of your choice, or to own your own weapon, are all examples of the value of individual freedom in action.

Most Americans assume that everyone in the world wants to be individualistic and independent. They find any other way of thinking hard to understand. When they meet people from Asia, Latin America, Africa or the Middle East who seem to be very concerned about the views of family, friends, or work colleagues, or who have a strong sense of obligation to the group, the culturally uninformed American is likely to see them as lacking self-confidence and as being overly dependent on what others think. To Asians, this American focus on individuality is often seen as opportunistic, selfish, and lacking concern for others.

Costs and benefits

Each approach, whether individual-centered or group-centered, has its costs and benefits. Those who grow up in a group-based, traditional Asian society grow up in a system of relationships which usually provides them with significant economic and emotional support. The extended family and its resources are there for them.

When hardships come, more often than not, there will be people who are willing and obliged to assist. For many in Asian societies, this provides tremendous psychological security and stability when they are in their family, friendship or work groups, a stability and security that individualistic Americans rarely have.

Many of the benefits that come from a group-based culture, come at the expense of the individual. To survive, the needs of the group have to come first. Individuals have to be willing to sacrifice their own needs and personal goals for the general interest of the group. People from group-based cultures must take into account the feelings, needs, and desires of all the members of their group, not just their own. There are many proverbs throughout Asia, like the one commonly heard in Japan and China, "The nail that stands up gets hammered down," or the Malay one, "The duck that quacks loudest will be the first to get shot," that remind people not to be too different or independent.

Americans, on the other hand, are generally freer to establish their own identities and to pursue their own goals, to live their lives, more or less, as they please. The costs, of course, can be tremendous. Many Americans experience isolation, insecurity, and loneliness. Others suffer under the burden of economic pressures and hardships which they must face alone. Still others, trapped by economic realities beyond their control, in situations which they cannot easily change, face criticism from their fellow Americans for failing to realize the American dream of being successful through individual effort.

The power of groups

While Americans, of course, are influenced greatly by the groups to which they belong, this influence traditionally has been less powerful than for people coming from Asian societies. In the traditional Asian village which has been our point of reference, the people you worked with were the same people with whom you lived, the same people with whom you prayed, socialized, and did business. For Americans, at least for the last few generations, the people in their extended families (relatives beyond parents, brothers and sisters) have not been the people with whom they worked, have been different from their friendship groups, and often have been different from the people in their religious or political groups.

The two systems may be represented as follows:

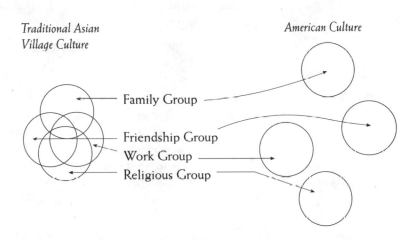

The overlapping groups in traditional Asian societies further strengthen the power of the family, village, or clan. For most Americans, no group holds the central place in their lives. Different groups exert different, often competing, influences. The American, therefore, is typically more independent of the groups to which he or she belongs and, as a result, is less concerned about maintaining smooth relationships.

Business Applications

Privacy/Confidentiality

Mr. Stein is visiting Sumatra for business consultations with the Indonesian affiliate of his company. His host, Mr. Suharto suggests they go out to the open-air night market, so Mr. Stein can sample Indonesian nightlife. Mr. Stein enthusiastically accepts this invitation, looking forward to getting a glimpse of "typical" Indonesian life. After only 30 minutes in the market, Mr. Stein is ready to return to his hotel. He didn't expect the crowds and finds the market's sights, sounds, and smells overwhelming. Mr. Suharto wonders what went wrong.

Americans need privacy

One logical outcome of American individualism is that Americans customarily have a strong sense of, and need for, personal privacy. On one level, this means that they need and demand more physical space around them — whether this be in their offices, their homes, or when driving their cars. On another level, this means that they like to have "psychological" space around them as well. Many Americans like the idea of having some private time each day — time when they are alone, just with themselves. They value this as time to think, read a book, or just to be away from the demands of anyone else. This is seen as positive, and something that helps individuals to maintain their mental health. Americans often assume everyone has similar needs for privacy.

You will see Americans' need for privacy displayed both on and off the job. For example, compared to the free flowing openness of an Indonesian village house or a Chinese or Korean farmhouse, where people can and do go into any room, the typical American home, whether in the country or the city, has doors for every room. If the family can afford it, each child has his or her own bedroom. American parents will knock before entering the bedroom of their teenager. It is the child's private territory and it is important for parents to respect their children's privacy.

When Americans go alone to a restaurant, they generally will sit at a table by themselves. When they get on a bus, they most likely will try to find a seat in a row that is unoccupied. Americans often will apologize for interfering with another's physical or psychological privacy. "Excuse me. Can I interrupt you?" Americans might ask, if you are working and they want to speak with you. They do this to respect your privacy. If they feel their privacy is not being respected, they will react by physically withdrawing or verbally becoming very abrupt. This means that they will give short answers to your questions and try to end the conversation as soon as possible.

Americans have a private zone, like a bubble of space around their bodies which is about 3 cm. deep. This private bubble shouldn't be broken by strangers. In a crowded elevator, for example, when people touch accidentally, the American generally will apologize. They will say "Sorry" or "Excuse me" to indicate they did not intentionally enter into someone's private space, but were forced by the circumstances to get closer than they normally would. Americans often feel uncomfortable initially with the press of bodies and the overwhelming number of sights and sounds on the streets of Asia. It is more than they are used to.

Privacy
at work
At work, the typical floor plan of an American office divides the work space into separate offices, so that individual privacy is maximized. If this is not possible, dividers are set up in the work area so that each person has his or her own space. American workers often will decorate their space with personal pictures, posters, or plants to individualize it further and to make it their own. Asian government offices, or businesses with a traditional orientation, are normally set up quite differently. There are no wall dividers between employees and the supervisor may have his desk in the middle or the back of a sea of other desks.

What This Means For You:

Americans will respect your privacy. They will knock before entering your office. They will ask if they can interrupt a conversation. They expect you to do the same with them.

Asian togetherness

In many Asian cultures, privacy is a luxury which few can afford. It is less important than a sense of togetherness. Doing things together and being with other people, sometimes lots of other people, is a positive experience for most Asians. For example, Asian restaurants, even expensive ones, are generally noisy, busy, crowded places. In contrast, expensive American restaurants are generally quiet, with low lights and great care taken to keep different groups of guests as separate and private as possible.

In many Asian languages, the word "privacy" does not exist. When it does, it often has a negative feel to it, communicating a sense of loneliness and isolation from the group. Privacy, as most Americans know and use it, is neither understood nor valued in most Asian societies.

In countries like Japan and Korea where population pressure is great and the lack of privacy inevitable, cultures have developed techniques for constructing imaginary walls of privacy around people that allow them privacy even while in public. A visitor does not "see" a person he has come to visit if that person is not ready to receive him. A cough by the visitor upon entering announces that the imaginary wall of privacy is about to come down.

Confidentiality

Americans are private about information as well. Unlike many Asian cultures where information is more generally shared within the group, Americans tend to restrict the flow of information to those for whom they think the information is directly relevant. Often, Americans have a broader definition (different glasses) of what types of information ought to be considered confidential than do their Asian counterparts. For example, information regarding the salary and benefits of a given individual, from an American perspective, clearly is confidential. This may not be the case in some Asian cultures. Americans get upset when they find that information they thought was private is known generally by the staff.

What This Means For You:

To be perceived as trustworthy by an American manager, do not share any information that has been conveyed to you confidentially with anyone else, without direct permission from the person who told you. Also, never gossip or talk to colleagues at work about other colleagues. This is one of the surest ways to get into trouble in an American company.

Self-Reliance/Hospitality

When an American is lost and looking at a map in an Asian city, it is not unusual for someone to come to his or her assistance. That person generally will give directions to the destination and, more often than not, if the destination is not far, walk the foreigner to the desired location. In an American city, people may be equally helpful. However, it would be very unusual for an American to accompany a foreigner to the destination, even if it is just around the block. Instead, the American will give verbal directions. The American assumes the foreigner neither needs nor wants any other type of assistance.

Americans are taught independence

From an early age Americans are raised to be independent. They are taught that only through individual effort can they make their way in the world. No one will take care of them. Most American parents try to raise their children to be responsible for themselves and their behavior. The idea is that children move from total dependence at birth to total independence in their late teens or early twenties, when most move from their parents' households to households of their own. The parents' role is to help their children prepare for a life of independence. It is not unusual for an American parent to ask a two-year old to decide what she wants for breakfast or to encourage a three-year old to dress himself. In general, American parents encourage their children to express their opinions, to make their own choices, and to do things for themselves.

One way you will see independence displayed at work is in the Americans' emphasis on having clear job descriptions and specifically defining tasks and responsibilities. Americans clearly separate their work responsibility from that of their colleagues. This gives them individual ownership, but also individual responsibility that is theirs and theirs alone.

Self-reliance: Doing things for yourself, by yourself

The value of independence produces another value, that of self-reliance. Self-reliance means not being dependent upon others. It means doing things for yourself, by yourself. "God helps those who help themselves" is an American proverb which reflects this value of not being dependent upon others. The typical (and much-joked about) American male driver would prefer to spend extra time trying to find his own way when lost, rather than to stop and ask for directions. Aging parents often prefer to live on their own, rather than to move in with their children. College students will take out personal loans, rather than ask their relatives to support them at university. America is sometimes called a "do-it-yourself" society. You will see high level managers at home on weekends mowing their own lawns, repairing their houses, and washing their own cars.

This does not mean that Americans never help each other. In fact, there is a strong tradition of neighbors helping each other and families pulling together, especially in times of crisis. What it does mean, however, is that when Americans need help, it is seen as their responsibility to ask for it.

Asians are taught to be interdependent

The American emphasis on self-reliance is very different from the emphasis of its counterpart in Asia of interdependence. In most Asian cultures, people are taught to depend and rely on the members of their families or groups. Things get done through the joint responsibility and cooperation of the members of the group. You need other people and they need you. Unlike American parents, traditional Asian parents take pride in being dependent upon their children in their old age. Often times, if it is possible, the members of Asian families live together, or near each other, each individual supporting and supported by the others. Interdependence and mutual assistance, such as the *gotong-royong* system in Indonesian and Malay villages or the *bayanihan* system in the Philippines is part of the very fabric of Asian society. You see it in the home, in schools, and in the workplace. It is one of the foundations of Asia's business success.

Mr. Leong, a senior salesman from his American company in Singapore, has been transferred to headquarters for six months to learn the latest sales techniques. His first week is spent in training to familiarize him with the latest approaches being used and to introduce him to his territory. After this, he is left on his own to develop his own plan and to implement it. Even though his American supervisor says, "Let me know if I can help you in any way," she rarely stops in to see him and to check on how he is doing. Mr. Leong feels unsupported, ignored, and pressured to make decisions by himself in areas where he is not knowledgeable. He wonders why he was so enthusiastic about coming to America.

If you need help or clarification

In business, American managers will typically assume you don't need help unless you ask for it. If you ask, they will be glad to give you assistance. To an American, to offer help when it is not wanted is to treat a person like a child or as an incompetent worker. Generally,

American managers go out of their way not to communicate this type of message to their colleagues or subordinates. The problem here is that Asian employees may be reluctant to ask an American manager or trainer for assistance or for further explanation. In Asian cultures, it can be difficult to admit to those in positions of authority that you need additional help, for fear of how you will be seen. The Asian manager often offers help without being asked. The American manager or trainer, while more than happy to assist if asked, often will not offer assistance, assuming that if an Asian employee needs help, he or she will ask. The result can be frustration; frustration on the part of the Asian because more assistance or clarification is not forthcoming and frustration on the part of the American who reasons, "If you wanted more help, why didn't you ask me for it!" As you can see, the potential for cross-cultural missing (misunderstanding) in this type of situation is high.

What This Means For You:

When in America, do not expect the same degree of hospitality or assistance that you would receive back home. By letting you do things on your own, Americans show their confidence in you. If you need extra help or clarification, ask for it clearly, directly and as soon as possible.

You fly into an American city to visit one of the company's processing plants. You are met at the airport by Mr. D'Angelo who drives you to the plant and accompanies you on the site visit. At the end of the day, you go out to the parking lot and Mr. D'Angelo gives you the keys to a company car, a map of the city and directions to your hotel. He then leaves.

Asian hospitality/ American hospitality

Another example of the self-reliance/interdependence difference occurs when an overseas guest visits the U.S. When Americans travel to Asia on business, they almost always are impressed with the hospitality and kindness of their Asian hosts. They are typically met at the airport, invited out to dinners, and generally find their needs are considered and often anticipated. When Asian hosts become guests in America, they may receive a very different type of welcome. They may or may not be met at the airport by their American hosts. They probably will be invited out to a business lunch, but may find they are left to fill their after-work time by themselves. The Americans are not being impolite, from an American point of view. They just have different cultural rules and assumptions about hospitality. They may assume that their Asian guests want to be independent and on their own. Also, they may assume that America really isn't such a hard place to figure out, and, if guests need help, they will ask. Thirdly, the American hosts may assume that their obligations to their guests end at the end of the work day. All of these assumptions are probably wrong from the perspective of most Asian guests, but they come from the core American values of self-reliance, privacy, and separation of work and personal life. These different cultural rules and glasses can make being a guest in the U.S.A. an unsettling experience for the Asian visitor.

What This Means For You:

Americans separate their "work life" from their "private life", that is, their family and friendships. After working hours, they are less likely to spend time socializing with people from the office than their Asian colleagues.

Personal Relationships at Work

A major American multinational is thinking of expanding into Indonesia. It has found a local partner and has carried out a series of negotiations to formalize the working relationship. On the first visit, Mr. Maddox, a senior vice-president, represented the company. On the second visit, a senior financial officer led the negotiating team to discuss financial issues. Succeeding visits were led by senior marketing, production and administrative specialists. The Americans thought they had "covered all the bases". They couldn't understand why the Indonesian company's management was so slow in making the final decisions. The Indonesians, on the other hand, were reluctant to finalize the deal because they didn't feel they knew any of the Americans well enough to trust them.

Asians are personal in business

Traditionally in Asian societies, it was inconceivable to have a business relationship with someone you didn't know, someone who wasn't somehow connected to you or to someone you knew. Asians in business are naturally team players. Success in business depends upon what your personal or business connections are like, as much as on your education, skills, or talent. Chinese call this important element of business *guanxi*, Japanese call it *kone*. In Korean it is *dong chang saeng* and in Indonesian it is *bapakism*. Things get done through and by the good relationships which business colleagues have with each other. These business relationships often have long histories and potentially long futures. They form an intertwining set of partnerships that carry with them mutual responsibilities and rewards. These relationships go beyond any one specific contract or sale. Today, personal relationships continue to be at the core of much of Asian business. Loyalty to the company or group remains important. The success or failure of the group becomes the success or failure of the individual. As in the family or village setting, relationships form the basis of economic survival and success in Asia.

*Americans
are
impersonal
in business*

Americans agree that relationships are always important in business. Nevertheless, most Americans do not need to have a long-term relationship with someone in order to do business with him or her. Because of America's urban, industrial history, and because of the high degree of mobility in the society (the average American moves every four to five years), Americans have learned to do business with people they do not know, even with people they may not like. To them, "business is business", and it has little to do with the other parts of their lives. The American company is not a family, but rather a workplace and profit-making organization. No one is indispensable and people can be replaced if they don't serve the needs of the company.

What This Means For You:

You can do business with an American without having a strong personal relationship. In a first meeting with an American manager, start the process by clearly stating your goals and what you want to achieve. Keep the focus on these goals. At the end of the meeting, summarize what has been agreed upon and the next steps to be taken by both sides. This will increase the American's confidence in you.

Americans often go on business trips to Asia, hoping to conduct business in three different countries in ten days. They plan to drop in, conclude an agreement, and then fly off to the next appointment. They often are mystified when they find it takes far longer to do business in Asia that they thought it would and that, without a relationship, little gets accomplished.

Ms. Martin walks quickly into the office as the work day is beginning. When she sees her Filipino colleague, Mr. Roxas, approaching, she holds up her hand and says, "Can't talk now! I've got some really important work to take care of." She rushes into her own office and closes the door. Mr. Roxas feels offended by Ms. Martin's bad manners.

Asians work at having good relationships

Traditionally, Asians in business have placed great emphasis on harmony and cooperation in the workplace. The work setting is like a large family. The needs and concerns of all must be taken into account. Feelings are important. Great care is taken to prevent public embarrassment or humiliation. Maintenance of harmony or the appearance of harmony is all-important. It is often more appropriate for things to appear right, than to actually be right.

In a group-based business environment, you must consult with others before you make significant decisions. Consensus becomes very important. It is equally important to make special efforts to ensure that the work environment is pleasant and conflict-free — at least on the surface. Asian managers spend considerable time and energy paying attention to relationships to ensure that this is the case.

Americans value relationships, but ...

Both Asians and Americans believe that maintaining good working relationships with employees, colleagues, and business contacts is important. Most Americans, however, believe it takes less to establish these relationships and less to keep them going. Americans often begin business meetings by getting "down to business" very quickly, with limited time to establish or re-establish relationships around the table. In times of stress, they may appear only to be concerned about getting the job done, focusing on the bottom line. To an Asian manager, this approach may seem cold or uncaring. While Americans like to have smooth and pleasant relationships at work, many do not believe, as most Asians do, that this is absolutely critical to success.

What This Means For You:

Americans, particularly when under stress, may neglect the small courtesies at work, such as saying "Good morning". Americans see these as polite gestures, nice to do, but not really critical. While this may be rude and uncaring from your perspective, try to remember that such behavior is not intended to offend you.

Speaking Your Mind

At a meeting attended by division managers for an American multinational held in an Asian capital, two supervisors, one American and one Asian, were both asked to present proposals for how they were going to meet their yearly sales forecast. When the American manager presented his proposal, there was little comment from the boss or other attendees. Then it was the Asian manager's turn. After his presentation, his American colleague suggested some ways in which he thought the Asian manager's plan could be improved. His intention was to help, to come up with the best possible marketing plan for the company. The result was that the Asian manager felt embarrassed.

Americans express their opinions

One result of the emphasis Americans place on individuality is that Americans, in general, are less concerned about what others may think of them than their Asian colleagues. Among American managers, you will note a much greater variety of opinions and a willingness to express them. Typically, in a meeting of Asian and American managers, the Americans end up dominating the meeting, if only by the volume of words they speak. Americans often will speak openly about things they like and dislike. If not expressed verbally, their emotional reaction to an idea or situation is often quite clear from their voice tone, gestures, and facial expressions. Unlike many of their colleagues from Asia, most Americans have not been taught to mask their emotional reactions. While they are taught to take into account the feelings, needs, and opinions of others, particularly those of their boss, the cultural demands for maintaining group harmony and consensus are far weaker than in most Asian societies. Americans may misunderstand when they observe Asian managers apparently agreeing publicly on some issues by not raising or defending alternative points of view, while privately disagreeing with them. They may interpret this behavior as being insincere or being unwilling to stand up for your beliefs.

> ### What This Means For You:
>
> *Americans may be critical of how things are done in your culture and not realize that such comments may be very offensive. Rather than become resentful, try to help the American, who may only be looking at the world through American cultural glasses, see how your culture makes sense.*

Americans are direct

Because Americans are, for the most part, less concerned about maintaining harmony, they are more likely to be direct and confrontational than their Asian colleagues.

There are many phrases like, "Don't beat around the bush" or "What's the bottom line?", that reflect this tendency to expect that people will be very clear and specific in stating what they think and want from others. Saying "no" directly isn't seen as rude. Instead, it is seen as necessary to prevent misunderstandings in the future. Often Asians see this type of behavior as offensive and disrespectful of human dignity. Americans often view Asian indirectness as dishonest or insincere. This is an area that has great potential for cross-cultural misunderstanding. Because it deserves in-depth discussion, we have devoted Chapter 10 to this, in addition to the material which follows.

Disagreement/Feedback

Two American colleagues get into a heated argument while discussing next year's business plan at a staff meeting. Voices are raised and each strongly defends his position. At the end of the meeting, one manager turns to the other and invites him to lunch. The Asians in the group are amazed how, after such a heated argument, these two can seemingly be friends again.

Americans agree to disagree

You will notice that, in a group meeting with Asian and American businesspeople, it is normally the Americans who are more likely to voice disagreements. Because of their education and upbringing, Americans are more willing to question or challenge an idea with which they disagree. Expressing differences of opinion in public is considered a healthy behavior. For most Asians, maintaining harmony is the higher goal. If you don't consciously work to maintain smooth interpersonal relations, you are lacking in integrity. You are self-centered and a bad influence on society.

Americans believe that if you criticize a person's ideas, you are not necessarily criticizing the person. Many Asians see no distinction between criticizing an idea and criticizing the person whose idea it is. When you criticize someone's idea, you are criticizing that person. Many Americans believe that you can separate the idea from the person. It is possible, if done correctly, for Americans to tell others they disagree with their ideas and not let that damage the relationship. As a matter of fact, it is perceived as cowardly and unprofessional not to voice your disagreement, especially if the topic is a critical one.

What This Means For You:

If you are uncomfortable with expressing disagreement in a meeting, but you have serious questions or concerns about the issues discussed, arrange to speak privately to the individual in charge about the issues as soon after the meeting as possible. Be sure to also explain why you did not raise these issues during the meeting.

"Constructive" criticism

Most Americans view feedback as an important management tool. By feedback, Americans mean either supportive words or observations which focus on the good work you are doing or corrective comments which focus on behavior that could be changed to make you more effective.

Generally, Americans believe that you should view your mistakes as opportunities to learn. They have developed the concept of "constructive criticism" — feedback that indicates a change of behavior is needed. The job of a supervisor includes discussing mistakes with those whom he or she supervises to ensure that these mistakes are not repeated. The best American managers criticize in private. Typically, criticism, once given, is over. The American manager moves on to the next task, issue, or concern. Ideally, the goal of feedback in American management, is not to hurt or embarrass you. Rather, it is to help you to be more effective in the future.

In many Asian cultures, criticism is seen as destructive. It embarrasses individuals and threatens the harmony of the group. Criticizing someone else is a reflection of bad manners, at best. At worst, it is a deliberate effort to offend and to cause harm.

Ms. Kerner, the General Manager of an American subsidiary in Indonesia, criticized Mr. Halim's recent performance at a staff meeting for failing to meet sales forecasts in the previous quarter. She wanted to begin a dialog so that staff could explore what went wrong and how to do better for the following quarter. She was surprised at how little discussion went on at the meeting. She did most of the talking. She was even more surprised when Mr. Halim resigned the following week. He felt he could no longer stay with the company. The loss of face was intolerable.

Face is less important to Americans

A factor that may explain the kind of painful cross-cultural misunderstanding described above revolves around the concept of face. Americans, like Asians, have "face". They don't like to be publicly embarrassed or humiliated. American managers generally go out of their way to maintain the dignity and respect of their employees, their colleagues, and themselves. However, in general, an American's concept of face is less developed than that of Asians. Also, given their individualistic cultural perspective, face is less important to them.

What This Means For You:

If your boss is critical of your work, try not to become discouraged. Do not assume that your boss does not like you. Instead, ask your boss for specific suggestions on how to improve your performance. Be sure you understand what is suggested, then try it. Go back for more advice if you continue to have difficulty.

To be honest or to be polite

For many Asians, the way things look may be as important or even more important than the way things are. How something is said or done may be more significant than what is actually said or done. For Americans, particularly in the work setting, truth is often thought to be more important than feelings or appearances. Americans often say, "Honesty is the best policy." They believe an answer or objective "truth" can be found to each management dilemma or decision. By facing reality squarely (openly and honestly), you can go on to solve almost any management problem.

In most Asian societies, it may well be the reverse, with Asian managers, at times, willing to forego short-term confrontation in the interest of maintaining long-term relationships and the psychological comfort of those involved. In general, Asians believe that, if forced to choose between the two, it is better to be polite than honest, in both personal and business relationships. For Americans this approach is more acceptable in one's personal life than on the job.

In American culture, it sometimes is acceptable to tell "white lies", untruths designed to protect another's feelings. However, this is only acceptable when the consequences of this type of response are not serious. Telling your neighbor that you enjoyed the meal she prepared for you, even when you disliked the food, is considered polite and expected behavior. In business, however, if forced to choose between being honest and being polite, Americans generally believe that it is better to be honest than to be polite, especially if it involves an issue of some importance.

Asians, of course, do give feedback to their colleagues, subordinates and superiors, but they usually do it in private or indirect ways, often using a third party. These ways are more subtle than those which the typical American is accustomed to. The problem here is that Americans may not know when they are being given feedback by an Asian manager or colleague. (Remember our concept of cultural glasses.) On the other hand, Asians may feel that feedback given to them by Americans is too harsh, too direct, and far too public.

Feedback Strategies That Work With Americans

If you are in a position where Americans report to you, sooner or later you will find it necessary to offer some feedback to them. Alternatively, if you are supervised by an American, you may find the following approaches are used with you.

When you want to support a behavior or activity:

1. Let the person know you are pleased with something he or she did.

2. Be specific and describe the behavior or event you observed.

3. Explain how the behavior made a difference to you or the organization.

4. Thank the person once again for the good performance.
    "I'm really pleased you finished the report on XYZ two days ahead of schedule. That gave me extra time to review it. Thanks, I really appreciated that."

When you want to point out an error or correct inappropriate or ineffective behavior:

1. Ask for a time to meet. Good timing is critical to ensure that the feedback is heard.
    "Bob, I'd like to talk to you about the XYZ report. When would be a good time today for us to get together?"

2. Describe the event or behavior in terms of specific, clearly observable facts.
"You turned the XYZ report in two days later than you said you would."

3. Describe the effect or result of the employee's action on you, the work group, or the organization.
"That meant that I didn't have enough time to fully review it before it went on to my supervisor."

4. Before assuming the employee is at fault, ask what happened. Really listen so you understand the issue.
"Bob, tell me what happened."

5. Define the expected or correct behavior for the employee, if appropriate.
"Bob, when we agree upon a deadline for a project, I need you to get it to me on time or to let me know beforehand if you're running into problems."

6. If appropriate, jointly develop an action plan to correct the mistake and to make sure it doesn't happen again in the future.
"Let's take a look at some of your time management techniques (or work load or ....) to see how you can avoid this problem next time."

7. State your confidence in the employee and his or her ability to handle similar situations in the future.
"Bob, I'm glad we had this talk. I'm much more comfortable now on this issue and don't think we'll have any problems with it in the future."

Conflict Resolution/Agreement Management

You have a conflict with a manager from another department who is older than you and who has been with the company longer than you. The conflict arises because the way she organizes the work for her department does not allow you and your staff time to get your work done. This makes you look bad. How do you handle it?

It is safe to say that no one from any culture likes conflict. However, conflict may have different meaning for Americans than it does for Asians. How it is viewed, managed, and resolved are subject to the cultural rules we follow and the cultural glasses we wear.

Conflict can bring positive change

For many American managers, a disagreement or conflict is not necessarily bad. While it is not something Americans ordinarily seek out, it is believed that conflict can be productive, if it brings up issues or problems that need to be addressed. American history is full of examples of positive benefits that have come out of conflict. The end of slavery, the civil rights movement, advances in women's rights, are examples of social improvements that have come out of conflict.

American managers typically believe that a healthy, developing organization is always growing and changing. New ideas or new ways of doing things will emerge and they will have to compete with each other for the organization's scarce resources. Conflict is the natural result of this process. Discussions, disagreements, and sometimes even arguments are necessary to determine what the best choice is among all the competing options.

Americans believe that most conflicts between people or within society can be resolved. What is needed is the commitment to find a solution that meets, at least in part, everyone's needs, and a clear understanding of the issues involved (the facts). When faced with a conflict, Americans like to get to its source. This means dealing directly with the person or persons involved to resolve the conflict. Americans talk about meeting problems or conflicts "head on" (being direct), getting the information "from the horse's mouth" (from those directly involved), and "laying your cards on the table" (sharing information).

What This Means For You:

If you have a conflict with an American colleague, try, first of all, to resolve it with that person directly. Americans only go to the boss to deal with a conflict they are having with another employee when they are unable to resolve it themselves. Going through an uninvolved colleague or outsider may be perceived as "sneaky" or cowardly.

The individual-centered perspective of Americans naturally causes them to see conflict in terms of winning and losing. "If I win, that means that someone else must lose." There is only one winner in a beauty contest, a car race, or a baseball game. Americans teach their children how to be good winners as well as how to be good losers.

Americans are taught conflict resolution strategies

In business, this win-lose perspective clearly does not work in the long term. Managers are taught, ideally, to look for win-win solutions to problems or disagreements, solutions which will benefit everyone in some way. While this may not be their normal cultural style, successful American managers can be quite effective in using conflict resolution strategies. Through discussion and compromise, a win-win solution or "third" solution — not my answer, not your answer, but an answer that meets both our needs — can be found. This is what American managers are trained to do in many of the teambuilding, conflict resolution, and supervisory seminars they attend. Many Asian managers seem to know how to do this naturally (actually, culturally).

For Asians, conflict is dangerous

For most Asians, conflict is seen as very dangerous and almost always destructive. Traditionally, in Asian societies where lack of mobility meant that people had no choice but to live together, and where their survival depended on their ability to cooperate with each other, there was a clear and powerful need to limit conflict. Historically, in rural village societies, when people fought or had serious disagreements, they were unable to work together in the fields to prevent famines, unable to harvest the benefits of a group-based social and economic system. Harmony, or the absence of conflict, became a dominant goal of most Asian cultures. Without it, society could not survive.

Asians use agreement management

As a result of this concern about the destructive influences of conflict, people in Asian societies developed and became very skilled at preventing conflict through processes of agreement management. Agreement management, which is very different from conflict resolution, includes those social behaviors designed to increase harmony and limit disagreement or conflict. These behaviors aim to prevent conflicts from occurring, rather than to deal with them once they have erupted. They include the many and varied forms of social etiquette used to give and preserve face. Agreement management works to prevent anyone from looking bad publicly or from being backed into a corner from which there is no escape. This is accomplished by avoiding open disagreement and by minimizing the communication of "bad news" (criticism, failure, mistakes) as much as possible. If bad news has to be communicated, it is often conveyed indirectly, through a respected third party (elder, supervisor, leader), which makes the message more acceptable. If conflict or disagreement can not be avoided, third parties not directly involved in the conflict often work behind the scenes to bring about an agreement. When such systems break down and conflict flares into the open, it can be very destructive.

What This Means For You:

If you find yourself in a conflict with an American, do not expect arguments which stress harmony, cooperation or avoidance of conflict to be effective. Expect the American to use arguments focusing on personal and company costs and benefits.

Americans don't know the rules of Asian agreement management

In dealing with Asians, Americans are quite often unaware when they break the rules of Asian agreement management. For example, they may be unaware that the way they give feedback can be as important as what they say. They may not realize when they have backed someone into a corner. They may not hear an Asian saying "no" indirectly. They may not be aware when a question they ask causes great discomfort. They are just problem-solving in their usual direct style, wearing their unique American cultural glasses and responding as they have been taught, with American cultural rules.

Because of their approach to conflict resolution, Americans usually want to confront an issue of disagreement or a problem directly. If an American asks to speak to you about a problem, follow the steps outlined below. Of course, you can also request such a meeting. If you do, be clear and specific in making the request. Ask for an appointment at a convenient time. You might begin by saying, "I'm having a problem with... Can we schedule a time this week to get together to talk about it?" Once an appointment is set, you again should follow the steps below to help ensure successful resolution of the conflict.

Steps Toward Conflict
Resolution With Americans

Before the meeting:
1. *Clarify the issue.*
    - Try to understand all aspects of the conflict. (What is the real problem?)
    - Try to understand the other person's position. (Are there other ways of looking at this?)

2. *Prepare your position*
    - Get the facts/document your viewpoint.
    - Rehearse what you are going to say.

When you meet:
1 *Present your viewpoint.*
    - State your position clearly and directly.
    - Focus on the facts.
    - Suggest a solution, but indicate it isn't the only solution you will accept.
      "One possible way this can be dealt with is ..."

2. *Listen.*
    - Acknowledge the other person's position/feelings. Let him/her know you understand and appreciate his/her viewpoint.
    - Question to make sure you understand all of the other person's issues.

3. *Try to agree on a solution.*
    - Look for a win-win solution — something you both can live with.
    - Develop a plan to implement the solution (timelines, specific action plan).

Self-Advancement/Competition

If an Asian is an expert at playing golf, he is likely to say, "I play a little golf." If an American has studied Japanese for one year at university, he is likely to say, "I speak Japanese."

American self-promotion

Americans often are seen by Asians as being inappropriately immodest, bragging, or boastful. At the same time, Americans often see Asians as being inappropriately modest. American managers frequently send Asian staff to assertiveness training courses to learn how to speak out more forcefully and to publicly affirm their achievements. They often misperceive Asian modesty as a lack of ability or as a lack of self-confidence.

Growing up in an individualistic society, Americans typically believe that their identity comes from their achievements. You are, to a great extent, the sum of your accomplishments. Americans are taught that it is appropriate to talk about their accomplishments. They believe that you are the best person to present yourself in a positive light. While they are raised to believe that it is important not to boast or brag, it is not seen as bragging when you let others know of your achievements. It is only when you do it too much or at the wrong time, that Americans believe you have gone too far. Generally, in Asian societies, it is seen as the responsibility of others in the group, not the individual, to present the strengths of a colleague. It is not surprising then, that many Asians are uncomfortable talking about their own accomplishments or the things they do well.

Asian modesty

For Asians, modesty or being humble (minimizing one's abilities or achievements) is also a way of protecting one's face. For example, if John says publicly that he is a pretty good basketball player, many Asians would be concerned that he would be setting himself up for a loss of face because the next time he plays basketball, he may not perform well. From an Asian perspective, it is safer to keep expectations low and surpass them, than to raise expectations and fail in meeting them. This prevents you from losing face. Most Americans, not having the same degree of concern about face as Asians, see more gains than drawbacks in what they might call "realistic self-promotion".

What This Means For You:

While it is acceptable to behave with typical Asian modesty in most business situations, there is one situation where, in an American company, it will hurt you. That is during performance appraisal reviews or annual job evaluations. At that time, it is important, even if difficult, to share your honest impressions of your achievements and accomplishments with your superior.

Miss Lee is attending an advanced business seminar at the company's headquarters in the U.S. with a number of colleagues from her home country. She is able to grasp the material faster than the others in her group and is ready to move on to new material. However, the rest of the group needs more review and practice. Her American instructor offers her the chance to go ahead on her own. Much to her instructor's puzzlement, Miss Lee declines.

Competition as a positive value

To most Americans, it is logical and desirable to move ahead at your own pace and, if your abilities outshine others in your group, to move past them. Miss Lee's decision to decline to move ahead of the group would not make much sense to many Americans. To most American managers, the world is competitive and being the best you can be is seen as a very positive character trait. Success is commonly defined in terms of personal achievement. In Asia, success is often measured in terms of harmony with the group and fulfilling appropriate roles in the family and at work.

If placed in the situation described above, many Asians would react just as Miss Lee did. They might be concerned that moving ahead of the others in the group would destroy group cooperation and harmony. They might be uncomfortable at being set apart from their colleagues. Many Japanese companies (and companies from other parts of Asia) do not give individual commissions to sales staff as American companies do. Instead, they pool the sales commissions for the entire team. Asian business is no stranger to competition between companies, industries, or nations. It is, however, less comfortable when that competition is within one's group.

Competition brings out the best

Americans are raised on competition and believe that competition brings out the best in each person. In American business, competition is seen as a major source of progress and prosperity. Through competition, the most talented rise to the top. Many American companies will motivate staff through sales competitions, giving cash awards or prizes to the individual employee who has sold the most cars in a month or who has written the most insurance contracts in a year.

Competition in American society starts early. Americans even have baby beauty contests. In sporting events as in business, Americans often say, "Let the best man win." This means that the outcome should be decided by who has the most skills, knowledge, experience or determination. In an individualistic society, you have only yourself to rely on. In most American businesses, where there is no guarantee of long-term employment, it is the responsibility of the individual to prove his or her worth to the company. By outperforming their colleagues, Americans get ahead.

You will see many job advertisements in American newspapers that begin with, "Looking for an aggressive, self-starter . . . ." By "aggressive", the employer means someone who is competitive, who looks for opportunities and doesn't just wait for them to appear. By "self-starter", the American employer means someone who is independent and self-reliant, someone who does not require lots of supervision.

Competition in business: Close the deal

Americans can be aggressive, high pressure business-people. They want to make the sale and get the agreement. They are reluctant to take "no" for an answer. They not only want clients, contractors and suppliers to say "yes", but they want them to agree immediately. They will use facts and logic as the first line of persuasion. If logic and data doesn't work, they may use "sweeteners" (quality discounts, money-back guarantees, etc.) or threats ("If you can't give me an answer today, I can't guarantee the price.")

Motivation

You are the boss. An employee has done an exceptionally good job on a project and you wish to acknowledge her extra effort. How would you do it?

Competition is just one of the ways Americans use to motivate employees to perform better. There are a number of other ways managers attempt to encourage their subordinates to work harder and more productively. Among them are:

- financial incentives (i.e. bonuses, pay raises),
- increased responsibility,
- public recognition (i.e. merit awards, praise),
- criticism or threats of punishment,
- special incentives (i.e. trips abroad, training opportunities).

Americans are motivated by individual recognition

Both Asian and American managers use all of the above to get the best from their employees. Asians and Americans are motivated by financial rewards such as pay raises or bonuses. However, there are some cultural tendencies (glasses and rules) that result in Americans using certain methods more frequently than others.

In a 1989 study of motivational incentives by the National Career Development Association, it was found that recognition of their individual achievement was the most important motivator for U.S. business managers. These findings have been confirmed in a number of studies where recognition for work accomplished consistently comes out as the strongest motivator for Americans. In an individualistic society like America, your achievements define who you are. For many working professionals, they are their résumé. That is why one's job is so important to an American. To have meaning, your accomplishments must be recognized by others. This is why Americans, perhaps more than any other Westerners, are so responsive to criticism or praise. Other significant motivators for Americans found in the 1989 study included increased job responsibility, possibilities for advancement, ability to influence others, having control over one's work, and, of course, financial incentives.

Motivators for Asians

In addition to financial incentives, Asians tend to be motivated by appeals to group loyalty or relationships. Incentives or benefits that come not only to themselves, but also to their work teams, company, or family can be strongly motivating. As we have seen, Asians tend to be more concerned with being accepted and having a sense of belonging, gaining respect from supervisors, colleagues, and subordinates than Americans. Enhancing an employee's "face" (taking him or her out to lunch, public recognition) is a strong motivational incentive in many Asian cultures.

Another motivator involves the use of shame. Questions like, "What will others think of us if you do not make an effort to change?" put group pressure on employees to improve their performance. For many Asians, the wish to avoid criticism or public embarrassment of themselves, their work group, or their company is a strong motivator.

Two students score exactly the same on a mathematics test. They both get a "B." The Asian student goes home and his mother may say, "Why didn't you get an 'A'? You'll have to study harder to bring your grade up." The American student's mom might say, "Good job! You're really doing much better in math. You've brought your grade up from a 'C'. I'm very proud of you."

Americans motivate through praise

One way Americans recognize accomplishments is through praise. To explore this, let's look at how Americans motivate their children. While you might see some American parents scolding, threatening, and even hitting their children at times, this is not thought to be the preferred mode of childrearing, by many Americans. Americans tend to say, "Catch them doing something good." This means acknowledging positive behavior and rewarding it. Americans believe you can motivate more effectively by promoting the positive rather than by punishing the negative. They believe that desired behavior or actions, rewarded, are more likely to be repeated. American managers are taught to compliment workers who have done a good job. Praise of the individual is an important motivating tool in the American workplace.

Asians use praise, but it is different

Asians too will give public praise, but for different reasons and with far less frequency than the typical American manager. Asians give praise to promote face; Americans praise to motivate performance. When an American manager praises an Asian colleague or subordinate, the Asian may feel uncomfortable. It may be embarrassing to be singled out and the employee may be concerned about how he or she will be viewed by others.

Americans often use what seems to be exaggeration to many Asians when they use praise, saying, for example, "You've done a great job! I don't know what we would have done without you!" When Americans use words like "fantastic" or "wonderful" to describe relatively minor accomplishments or events, it may appear hollow and superficial to Asians. When asked what they think of Americans' use of praise, many Asians typically respond,

"She must not mean it," or "How can he be so positive about so many things all the time?" Most Asians are not used to the frequency or style of American compliments.

Americans, on the other hand, may feel uncomfortable without a generous helping of praise on a regular basis. Without it, they may wonder whether they are doing a good job or whether they are really being appreciated by their boss.

> **What This Means For You:**
>
> *If you are supervising Americans, it is important to compliment them more than you would those from your own culture.*

American trainer:	*"Sharifah, your work in class is really improving. I'm very pleased."*
Sharifah:	*(looking down) "Oh no, sir. My work is not very good at all."*
American trainer:	*"What do you mean by that? You've been number one in class for the last two weeks."*
Sharifah:	*(looking very uncomfortable now) "No, sir, I am not a good student."*
American trainer:	*"But Sharifah, you've made real progress in this training. You should be proud of how much you've learned in such a short period of time."*
Sharifah:	*"It is because you are such a good teacher, not because I am a good student."*
American trainer:	*"Well . . . . If you say so."*
	(The American trainer is really confused by this conversation. He wonders why Sharifah thinks she isn't a good student. He wonders whether he may have misjudged her.)

Responding to praise

The typical Asian response to a compliment from an American supervisor is a denial of that compliment, "I'm just doing my job." The Asian employee is being appropriately modest and humble. Responding in any other way to this type of praise is out of the cultural comfort zone of many Asians. Americans, however, are not used to people denying or disagreeing with compliments.

What This Means For You:

If you are praised by an American, the most appropriate response is to look him or her in the eye and just say, "Thank you."

The thousand-faced boss

Asians sometimes think of American managers as being "thousand-faced bosses." Americans can be very positive and complimentary of your efforts and achievements one day and the next day be very critical of a piece of work you have done. This can be most puzzling and frustrating. It only makes sense when you remember that:

1) American managers focus on the bottom line i.e. getting the job done.
2) Their individualistic culture has taught them to be direct in giving feedback.
3) In criticizing your work, they are not meaning to criticize you as a person.
4) When they see performance they like, they have been taught to reward it immediately and verbally.

Only then, will the American style of interaction with Asian colleagues begin to make sense.

6
The Informal American

Cultures in Contrast: Equality vs. Hierarchy

First impressions

First impressions are very important. Your initial impression of another person sets the stage for how you will think about and act towards that person. It gives you cues as to where someone "fits". What Americans typically look for in a first impression is to learn about the person as an individual and to determine if there is a sense of comfort or compatibility. In initial conversations, Americans look for common ground by talking about areas of potential mutual interest (sports, business, even the weather) or by telling stories about themselves and their families. When meeting someone new, they will ask such questions as, "What do you do?" "Where are you from?" "Do you have children? How old are they?"

> **What This Means For You:**
>
> *The initial ten seconds of meeting someone creates a vital first impression that affects how the person will view you. To be perceived as self-confident, honest and trustworthy by an American, shake hands with a firm grip, looking him or her directly in the eye as you do so.*

*Business
cards*

When American businesspeople visit Asia, one of the things they are always told is the importance of business cards. They often come prepared with boxes of cards in English and the local language. While many follow the ritual involved in exchanging business cards in Asia, many more miss the significance of what is really happening during the exchange.

In America, businesspeople exchange cards, but not as often and with nowhere near the formality of the business card exchange in Asia. To Americans, a business card is a helpful reminder of a name and a telephone number, if they need to contact that person at a future date. Usually, Americans barely glance at the business card they receive, looking at the name so they can pronounce it correctly. They may even write notes on the back of a card to remind themselves of items for follow-up or to summarize the discussion.

In Asia, the business card ritual has a different meaning. Business cards themselves provide a critical first impression. Asians handle them with much more respect than their American counterparts, seeing the card as a representative of the person and his or her company. Asians will certainly look at the name, but they most often will pay special attention to the title, noting the person's position. This provides the critical cues an Asian is looking for in knowing how to respond to the other person. As a first impression, Asians generally are more interested in knowing where you fit and with whom you are connected.

> *". . . all men are created equal."*
>
> — *United States Declaration of Independence*

> *"Among mankind, there are necessarily differences in elevations; it is impossible to bring about universal equality."*
>
> — *I Ching (Chinese classic)*

Asian cultures are hierarchical

Traditionally, in most Asian cultures, the belief that people are not, and cannot be, of equal rank, status, and authority has been accepted as reality. There are higher and lower positions in society. The social system is hierarchical, like a ladder with many steps. Older people have traditionally been treated differently from younger people, men from women, royalty from the common folk. In English, there is only one word for "you". In Japanese, Thai, and other Asian languages, there are at least ten or more words for "you", depending on age, status, role, sex, or relationship. Many Asian languages don't have words for "brother" or "sister". Instead, they have words for "elder brother" or "younger brother", "elder sister" or "younger sister" to reflect the different status that age brings. Thai twins born minutes apart refer to each other in older/younger brother or sister terms (Fieg, 1989).

Ideally, those in higher positions are expected to act with virtue and to take into account the needs of those below them. Those in lower positions are expected to be loyal and to obey their superiors. In exchange, they obtain support and assistance from those above them. If all follow the rules of their position or status, then society will be stable and prosperous. All will benefit.

Asians are comfortable with status differences

Asians, in general, are comfortable with hierarchical or vertical relationships. That is, by knowing their position on society's ladder, they know what to expect and how to respond to those above them and those below them. These ritualized rules for dealing with others provide a tremendous amount of predictability and security to human interaction. They help prevent embarrassment and discomfort. Asians are taught from birth how to comfortably style-switch (change how they respond) when dealing with people of higher and lower rank than themselves.

Asians typically excel at teamwork. Within a group, unequal status is considered natural. It is taken for granted that some will give directions which others will follow. When ten men move a heavy load, they work together smoothly as a unit. One person, the leader, determines what each should do and they do it with ease and cooperation.

American culture emphasizes equality

Americans approach the issue of relating to others very differently. They are most comfortable with relationships among equals. Historically and culturally, many early Americans left behind the feudal system of Europe with its emphasis on titles, position, and status. They came to a new country where they were judged by what they accomplished, not by the family to which they were born. Most Americans believe that no one is born better than anyone else. If you reach a higher position in life, it is because of your own hard work and effort. They emphasize a concept they call "equality of opportunity". This means that each person should have an equal chance of participating economically.

In reality, some Americans have a better chance of getting ahead than other Americans. Children of wealthy or even middle class parents have more opportunities than children of poor families. Many black Americans have fewer opportunities than the average white American. While it is clear that equality has not always been put into practice, the concept has been, and remains to this day, a strong cultural value and American ideal. As such, it strongly affects Americans in their everyday lives and decisions.

Business Applications

Equal Opportunity

Mr. Saito, the manager of a Japanese-owned company in America, thought things were going quite well. After a slow start, production was up, quality was improving, and the market for his product was expanding. He was quite surprised when he received notice that he and his company were being sued (taken to court) by one of his middle level women managers for sex discrimination. This employee felt that she had been passed over for promotion by management in favor of a male who had less experience and time with the company. She went to her lawyer before going to Mr. Saito.

All people treated the same

Because of their strong value of equality Americans generally believe that no favoritism should be shown or special benefits given because of position, connection, or friendship. Over the last forty years in America, a wide range of laws have been passed to confront racism and prejudice and to try to ensure that equal opportunity exists. Americans have great difficulty with what they call a "double standard" in which one person or group of people is treated differently from the others. They see this as a potential cause of great problems. While equality and justice have not always been the case in American history, it is commonly believed by most Americans that rules should be equally applied to everyone. For Asians, starting on the assumption that all people are not, and cannot be, equal, treating people differently is not inappropriate nor likely to cause problems, but necessary and logical.

In American business, for legal as well as cultural reasons, managers generally will go out of their way to ensure equal oppportunity in the hiring and promotion process. They strive to make it open to all, with the criteria being objective and clear. American society, through special programs and laws (i.e. affirmative action), promotes those in certain sectors of the society (women and minorities) who previously have not been allowed access into the ranks of management.

*Business
decisions
based on
merit*

Equality also comes into play when awarding contracts or making purchases. Americans in business expect decisions to be made based on the merits of a bid or proposal. That is, they expect people to have an equal chance to compete. Most American companies have detailed policies governing their purchasing or contracting practices to ensure that this is the case. Factors such as price, quality, service and supply are all considered important factors to take into account. To award a contract or to do business primarily on the basis of family or friendship connections is not only viewed as unfair, but as unethical.

What This Means For You:

If you are in a position to hire, promote, purchase, or contract, be sure you know your company's policies and that your decisions are defensible based upon objective criteria.

Status

At the conclusion of a three week seminar for a group of Korean managers preparing to go to the U.S., there was to be a graduation party. The senior American and Korean company managers, the trainees, their colleagues, and their families were to attend. The trainees were asked to select a representative to give a speech in English at that event. The American trainers assumed the speaker chosen would be the trainee who was most fluent in English. Instead, the group chose the most senior trainee, even though his English was very poor.

*Americans
can change
their status
in society*

In traditional Asian societies, the position into which you were born usually was the one you would hold for your entire life. Americans, at least white, middle-class Americans, see themselves as born with opportunity, but without a specific position in society. The position or status they achieve will depend on their own personal efforts. For the majority of Americans, status differences can and do change. It has been the experience of literally millions of immigrants to the U.S. to arrive with very little and to be able to better their position, to improve their status. American movies, novels, and folk tales are full of stories of the "poor boy who makes good", the person who starts out in a lowly position but who, through his or her efforts, overcomes obstacles to achieve economic and social success. These different cultural environments make for a dramatically different way of looking at relationships, where you fit in the social order, and how to treat others.

Asians generally expect and accept that in relationships, one person will be of higher status than the others. Americans, on the other hand, usually feel more comfortable in relationships between people of equal or near-equal status. In fact, Americans both dislike and distrust unequal relationships. They will feel resentful and are likely to rebel when not treated as an equal, even if they are of lower status. They also tend to feel somewhat uncomfortable when deferred to or treated as if they have a higher status.

Americans in Asia

When American executives move to Asia, they are often uncomfortable with the high status and deference paid to them. It is a new experience. They may try to minimize status differences or, in some cases, they may "let it go to their heads", and think themselves more important than they are. Asian cultural rules on how to treat people of different rank are new to them.

Americans minimize status differences

Americans have been taught to treat all people alike (even though in practice they don't follow this cultural ideal all the time). They usually avoid, if they can, treating other Americans as superior to themselves. To do so would be to put themselves in an inferior position. To be treated as an inferior is almost intolerable to the average American. One of the most damaging things one American can say about another is, "He acts as if he thinks he is better than we are." The American boss attempts to minimize status differences by playing on the company softball team to show he is "one of the guys", by having her staff call her by her first name, and by maintaining an "open door" policy towards complaints or criticism.

Asians visiting America

Typically, highly educated, professional people are treated with much greater respect in Asia than in the United States. One of the more difficult experiences for Asian business executives visiting the U.S.A. for the first time is how they may be treated by Americans in service occupations, such as hotel personnel or taxi drivers. Used to a certain amount of deference from service people back home, they may not expect to be treated as a social equal. If you visit America, a waitress in a restaurant may introduce herself by saying, "Hi, I'm Ann. How are you today?" A taxi driver may say, "How ya doing, Buddy?" and then strike up a conversation or offer his opinion on a range of topics from world politics to Asians in America. It is important to realize they are treating you just as they would treat any American.

What This Means For You:

Avoid acting in ways that may be seen by Americans as either arrogant and superior or submissive and inferior. To make a good impression, treat Americans as your social equals.

Equality means getting your hands dirty when necessary

One of the typical American behaviors which Asians often note with amazement and amusement when visiting America, is the willingness of managers to "get their hands dirty". In Asia, if you are university-educated and hold a high status management position, it is typically thought to be below your status or dignity to do manual labor or other jobs reserved for people of lesser status, pay, or education. Americans, coming from a culture that emphasizes self-reliance, equality, and getting the job done, whatever it takes, are more likely to engage in a necessary task, whether it fits into their job description or not. You may see American managers getting coffee for their guests, carrying chairs into a room for a meeting, or making their own photocopies.

Equality also means that, in conducting business, you may deal with someone much younger or of less status than yourself. To an American, concern about rank and hierarchy is not nearly as important as getting the job done. If you are good at what you do, regardless of your age or seniority, you are likely to get ahead. In negotiations or business meetings with Americans, there may not be the clear hierarchy that you are used to with Asians. Junior members on the American team may give their personal opinions. These same junior members may even express (perhaps non-verbally) their disagreement with the team leader.

What This Means For You:

Do not feel insulted if you do not automatically receive respect from an American colleague because of your position, age or seniority. You get respect in the American workplace largely through demonstrated accomplishments.

Status differences, American-style

This doesn't mean that there aren't status differences in American society or American business. Of course, there are. The difference is a matter of degree. The distinction between those of high status (the ruler, the boss, the teacher) and those of lower status (the subject, the employee, the student) is not as great in the U.S.A. as it is in Asian countries. Americans deliberately attempt to minimize status differences. The English language, unlike many Asian languages, does not have different pronouns (I, you, he, she, etc.) to convey status differences or different tones to communicate respect. It lacks the extensive vocabulary of many Asian languages that shows deference to those in positions of authority.

How status differences are reflected or how respect is shown in the American culture may not be obvious to the observer from an Asian culture (different rules and glasses, once again). The American blue collar worker, for example, may drive a fancy automobile, live in a large house, or dress in expensive clothes. Nevertheless, status differences do exist. In the workplace, the size and position of one's office and whether or not it has a window reflect status differences. (Large corner offices with windows generally go to those of highest status.) Likewise, who initiates conversation and who has the first or last word at a meeting are also indicators of who has the higher status position in a group of American businesspeople. Asian managers need to pay attention to and learn to read the American cultural cues regarding status.

Informality

An American trainer opened her training session for a group of Asian managers by sharing some jokes. Her goal was to "loosen up the group" and make everyone comfortable for the hard work that was to come. The Asian audience saw the trainer's behavior as a signal that they need not take the training too seriously. When they continued joking and talking to each other after the trainer "got down to business", she became angry with the group. She felt they weren't respecting her and she could not understand why they were not taking the training seriously.

Informality as a form of social oil

One way Americans manage status differences is through informality. This causes Americans to be seen by much of the world as open, approachable, and friendly. It also causes them to be seen as overly casual and, at times, disrespectful of those in positions of power or authority.

Asians are likely to engage in polite ritualized behavior, adjusting both to the formality of the occasion and to the status of the person, as their preferred style of dealing with others. Americans, on the other hand, are more attracted to informality. For most Asians, the observance of social formalities is extremely important. These formalities reinforce and maintain a sense of order and predictability in human interaction. Formal greetings, deference in speaking, sitting, eating, and other forms of polite behavior are all appropriate forms of recognition for high status members of society.

Americans see formality and protocol quite differently. They often view these behaviors as unnecessary, self-important, and as distancing people from one another. American managers often go out of their way to minimize status differences at work through informality. Informality is the social oil in American society that allows people to work together harmoniously.

Use of first names promotes informality

While Asians are used to being called by their title (Director Kim, Engineer Mohamed), Americans generally are more comfortable being called by their first names. In American culture employees frequently can be on a first name basis with their boss. The senior American manager who asks you to call him by his first name, who loosens his tie and puts his feet up on the desk while talking to you, who chats with the office boy as well as the executive, is trying to create an atmosphere of informality and equality. Americans believe this atmosphere will create the most productive working environment. They often do not see how these or similar actions might offend Asian colleagues or business contacts. In America, you "roll up your sleeves" to get the job done, dispensing with formality. In Asia, high status people usually do not take off their jackets or ties or eat a sandwich at a business meeting. Subordinates generally do not interrupt or disagree with their superiors or make jokes during contract negotiations.

What This Means For You:

Americans believe you can be informal, have fun, and still get the job done. Don't mistake American informality for lack of seriousness.

American informality is often interpreted through Asian eyes as a lack of respect or lack of appropriate seriousness of purpose for the task at hand. If an American is casually dressed or has a relaxed style in meetings, Asians may misinterpret this as not paying attention, being disinterested, or lacking respect and sincerity. The American may be seen as too loose, too casual, too friendly.

What This Means For You:

When American colleagues from the home office visit you in Asia, they may need to be reminded of the importance of formality and paying appropriate deference and respect when visiting government officials and other Asian businesspeople. Some tips on how to do this will be appreciated. Americans do not want to give offense or limit the chances of successful completion of their mission in Asia.

"Superficial" friendliness

Americans are often accused by Asians of being "superficially" friendly. That is, they are warm, open, and easy to connect with on the surface, but they are not really interested in developing true friendships, as Asians know them. Asians often mistake American friendliness ("Hi, How are you?" "Have a nice day," "Let's have lunch some time,") for friendship. They end up feeling disappointed when Americans don't follow through on their initial expressions of friendliness. Americans do have deep and warm friendships, but that type of friendship is usually something different from the friendliness they exhibit at work. Friendliness at work is meant to keep relationships smooth and to develop a positive working atmosphere. It communicates, "You are in my social network and we have a relationship that allows us to work comfortably together." Americans believe that warmth, informality and friendliness make everything go smoothly. (Asians, too, want harmony and smooth working relationships, but how you get there, what you say and how you say it, is different.)

Friendliness to the typical American is a form of "social oil" that takes the rough edges off American individualism and competition and allows people to work together harmoniously and effectively. Americans, on average, move fourteen times in their lifetime. Friendliness allows them to meet people quickly in a new environment. It communicates, "I'm not better than you. We're all in this together." Americans believe you don't have to be friends to get the job done, but Americans are encouraged to sound like friends.

What This Means For You:

Generally, if Americans really want to have a friendship with you, they will invite you to do things with them outside of office hours. Otherwise, their friendliness means they want to be able to work well with you, but do not want a deeper relationship.

Americans like to be liked

Americans view themselves as warm, open, accepting people and are surprised when others see them differently. They view themselves as generous and giving to those in need. They are somewhat offended when non-Americans point to the materialism and competitiveness in American society. Americans like to be liked. It is important that others have a good opinion of them personally and of America in general. You see this desire to be liked and accepted demonstrated daily in the American office through the ready smile, the casual comment to everyone passed in the halls, and the positive reaction to praise.

For many Americans, self-esteem, or feeling good about yourself, appears to be tied to social acceptance or approval from others. One possible explanation for this is that in an extremely individualistic culture, there is no group (other than, for many, their immediate families) which automatically offers acceptance and approval. To get approval, you have to seek it from others. Therefore, the opinion of others becomes important in developing a positive sense of yourself.

In some ways, this desire to be liked is contradictory to the points raised in the previous chapter where we discussed independence and individuality, traits that push Americans not to care about what others think of them, their ideas, or their behavior. The reality is, both are parts of the American character. The average American is more dependent upon others' acceptance and approval than he or she would like to admit. Independence, individuality, and self-reliance are values that are not always put into practice. On a day-to-day basis, maintaining approval of friends and colleagues — keeping things smooth — is valued by most Americans. When the issue is an important one, however, especially one which relates to concepts of "right" and "wrong", Americans have been taught to act on their value of independence, even in the face of disapproval from others.

American Humor

One way informality is expressed is through humor. Americans view humor as a way to "break the ice", to make people feel comfortable, and as a way to establish and maintain a friendly atmosphere. Americans frequently advise each other to spice up presentations and meetings with humor. They make a lot of jokes about themselves and others. It is a way of leveling the social scene, a way of saying we are all equal and shouldn't take ourselves, our positions, or our status, too seriously. Americans are famous for their teasing or personal joking which usually is intended in the spirit of fun, but which may be heard by an Asian colleague as a form of criticism. No one, whether the boss, president of the company, or President of the United States, is immune to humor.

Responding to jokes

A lot of humor in America, as in Asia, revolves around puns or word play. It can be very uncomfortable when everyone around you "gets" the joke but you don't see anything at all funny in what was said. You can laugh with everyone else (and feel uncomfortable) or not respond at all (and feel uncomfortable). There really aren't any good responses in this situation except to realize that humor is the last thing you understand about another culture. When you can understand jokes in another language you have truly become familiar with that culture.

Mr. O'Leary had been in Hong Kong for two months. Things seemed to be going very well. While waiting for the last few members of the staff to assemble for the weekly staff meeting, Mr. O'Leary, with a smile on his face, turned to his assistant, Mr. J.R. Lai and said, "J.R., that's the ugliest tie I've ever seen. Where did you ever find it?" Mr. Lai was speechless. He never expected his boss to notice his tie, but, if he didn't like it, he never expected Mr. O'Leary to say so in such a public way. Mr. O'Leary knew immediately he had made a mistake. He never meant to cause offense. But it was too late to take his words back.

Friendly sarcasm

Related to humor is something that really doesn't have a name, but which is very common. We call it "friendly sarcasm". Friendly sarcasm, or being negative about someone without really meaning it, is a very common form of interaction, particularly among American males.

Sometimes, it takes the form of saying to someone the opposite of what you really mean. A colleague might comment, "You didn't work very hard today," after you just put in a twelve-hour day. Usually, the American receiving such a comment will reply with an equal amount of friendly sarcasm. The colleague in the example given might say, "I just didn't want to make you look bad!" as a sarcastic reply.

For many Americans, this pattern of interacting communicates, "I have a good enough relationship with you that I can say something terrible about you and you'll know I'm just joking." It is a way of communicating that you are in my social group and that we are more friends than acquaintances.

Unfortunately, friendly sarcasm almost never works with Asians. The natural reaction of most Asians is one of astonishment and hurt. "How could anyone be so blunt, so rude, so uncaring of another's feelings?" Many Americans know this form of humor doesn't work with Asians and they try to avoid it. Still, for others, it is a hard habit to break. It is quite likely that if you work with Americans, you will experience this type of comment. When it happens, remember the concept of different cultural rules and glasses, even though your stomach may be in knots.

What This Means For You:

If someone uses "friendly sarcasm" with you, you have two choices. You can reply with the same kind of comment. This will encourage the person to use friendly sarcasm with you in the future. Or, you can say something like, "Excuse me?" This will let the Americans know that their attempt at this form of humor did not work. It is likely that they will apologize or tell you they were only joking. Even though you may feel upset, try to believe them. This response should help to discourage them from using this approach with you in the future.

Section III: Getting the Job Done

7

The Take-Charge American

Cultures in Contrast: "Doing" vs. "People" Orientation

"If at first you don't succeed, try, try again."

"You can do anything you want, if you want it bad enough."

"Take the bull by the horns"

— *American proverbs*

Americans are action-oriented

In the early 1990's, a very popular slogan from one of America's well known athletic shoe companies was, "Just Do It!" American history and culture are filled with examples of achievement. Americans see themselves as doers, people who can and will accomplish things. They talk about being "masters of their own destinies", meaning through their efforts and hard work, they can make things better for themselves and society. They are proud of having built their country up from an untamed wilderness in just a little over two hundred years.

Americans believe they should be doing something most of the time. Being active and involved in a task is highly valued. American managers are trained to make things happen. They often say, only half jokingly, "Don't just stand there, do something . . . Anything!!" Conversely, not being busy, active, or energetic marks you as a "loser" in American society. Americans get restless and impatient when they are not active. In a meeting of Asian and American businesspeople, for example, it almost always will be the Americans who fill in the silences. They are uncomfortable with what they see as the absence of productive action, the pauses in the conversation. They see pauses as breaks in the communication process rather than as a useful part of that process. Even recreation for Americans usually involves planning an activity, going somewhere, and doing something.

Asians, too, like to achieve things. However, as we have seen previously, group-based cultures may have other priorities. The process (how things get done) may be more important than the end result (what gets done). Establishing and maintaining positive interpersonal relationships are very important. It therefore becomes legitimate to sit and talk with others for hours and seemingly accomplish nothing — no contracts signed, no sales made, no action plans developed. The payoff comes in the relationship and the investment is long term. For many Asians, thinking, listening, and building relationships may be as, or even more, valuable than doing; caring about people, or just being, may be preferable to action.

Business Applications

Getting Results

Ms. Hunt supervises a number of Thai managers. She senses that all is not going well, but is not clear as to what the real issues are. She invites three of her senior managers to meet with her to get to the root of the problem. She senses it has something to do with her management style and asks for feedback. With practically no eye contact and a great sense of embarrassment, the managers respond by saying there is no problem. They avoid or deflect Ms. Hunt's other questions on the subject. Ms. Hunt leaves the meeting feeling frustrated that she couldn't get to the bottom of the problem. Her Thai managers leave feeling embarrassed that they were put in this situation.

Americans see themselves as "doers"

An American tends to judge colleagues or subordinates by what they accomplish rather than by who they know, what schools they attended, or their personal or family connections. When Americans meet each other, one of their first questions is, "What do you do?" They are asking, what is your job? How do you spend your time productively? They ask each other, "How are you doing?" and often inquire of a youngster, "What do you want to do when you grow up?" One of the highest compliments you can pay to an American worker is, "She gets the job done."

The majority of Americans believe that most problems, economic as well as social, can be overcome by hard work and creative thinking. The world, for most American managers, is a series of challenges or problems to be overcome. For every problem, there is a solution. They tend to view themselves first and foremost as problem-solvers. This "can-do" attitude is a source of pride and inspiration. It traditionally has given Americans a sense of optimism about any task they take on and about their country in general.

Americans are concerned about control — predicting and influencing events. Because of this perspective, American managers place great value on having an accurate flow of information, planning and anticipating problems, and being able to think creatively when problems arise. Their approach will be direct and, at times, confrontational, as they try to "get to the bottom of" (figure out) a puzzling situation.

Americans are impatient

This focus on results causes Americans to be very frustrated by bureaucracy or what they call "red tape". They view protocol and bureaucracy as the enemies of productivity, a waste of time and diverting energy from work to be done. Generally, they are impatient with anything that slows down the pace of getting the task accomplished.

The importance of the bottom line

The bottom line — getting results — is what counts to most American businesspeople. It is the primary measure of success or failure. They use words like, "in the final analysis" or "at the end of the day" to signify that their primary focus is on getting the job done. In American business, your performance appraisal will be based primarily upon what you achieve and how quickly you achieve it.

What This Means For You:

In a business discussion with an American colleague, focus on the bottom line — the task you both want to accomplish. Present your ideas in a factual and logical manner, pointing out clearly why the path of action you propose will achieve the desired results.

The top priority: Getting results

In contrast, many Asian cultures, with a strong emphasis on group harmony, place a higher value upon smooth interpersonal relationships. Americans also like to have smooth working relationships, but if pushed to decide between getting the job done and ensuring harmony and good feelings among colleagues, they almost always will choose getting results.

Performance Appraisals

Mr. Farris has worked in Malaysia for just over a year. He directly supervises Mr. Chin Sheau Ching, another recent addition to the management team of the American multinational company. Mr. Farris and Mr. Chin get along well. In fact, Mr. Farris went to Mr. Chin's house for Chinese New Year celebrations just two weeks ago.

The company requires an annual performance appraisal. Mr. Farris is aware that Mr. Chin has not followed through on some significant projects in the last year. In a one-on-one meeting, he discusses these areas of concern and suggests how Mr. Chin might improve his performance. Mr. Chin wonders how his boss can be so direct and rude. He thought the relationship was going just fine.

Why performance appraisals

In an attempt to make the best use of human resources in an organization, American managers usually rely on performance appraisals to measure results at work. Those who contribute the most, Americans believe, are the ones who should be rewarded. Those who fail to perform well, or who are unsuited for the position they hold, should be removed. American management believes that periodic reviews that are documented (written down) and quantified (backed up by figures, numbers, statistics) provide the best and fairest basis for making administrative decisions (promotions, pay raises, etc.). They see this feedback as essential for employee development. While giving this feedback is often uncomfortable for American supervisors, performance appraisals are considered a "necessary evil" to promote development of their staff and ensure quality performance.

Regular and standardized performance appraisals allow managers to make objective decisions (not clouded by feelings or relationship to the person) and to treat all staff fairly and equally. The result of this type of appraisal process is that: 1) personal considerations are minimized in job reviews; 2) younger, better performing managers may be promoted over older, more senior ones; and 3) loyalty and hard work become less important in job advancement than achieving measurable results.

American-style performance appraisals are particularly difficult for Asian managers. They demand perspectives and behavior that are neither typical nor comfortable for the average Asian manager. These include the ability to verbalize to your supervisor your strengths and successes and to receive direct feedback and criticism. The performance appraisal process, unless it is done very well, can be contrary to the Asian values of maintaining harmony and preserving face. The reality, however, is that this type of evaluation is a fact of life in most multinational companies.

How to Win at American Performance Appraisals

American-style job reviews can be very uncomfortable for the Asian staff. If they are a part of your professional life, here are some suggestions on how to make them work for you:

1. **Look at the evaluation as an opportunity to improve.**
   Although often not pleasant, try to view the experience as the chance to get needed information which will help you be more successful.

2.   **Come prepared.**
Think through your areas of demonstrated accomplishment and areas where you may not have done your best.

3.   **Bring the right attitude.**
Recognize that we all can learn to be more effective. Be positive about your ability to correct anything that has not been satisfactory. Remind yourself of the American manager's goals and the purpose of the job review — to better your performance, not to make you feel bad.

4.   **Acknowledge your successes.**
While contrary to the teachings of most Asian cultures, this is an important time to share your strengths and achievements. If possible, back them up with data, statistics, and other objective measures.

5.   **Accept responsibility for mistakes or shortcomings.**
Acknowledge the feedback, if you think it is legitimate. Don't give an excuse for something that went wrong. Don't blame others for your shortcomings.

6.   **Plan to do better.**
Discuss with your supervisor specific actions you can take or training you can attend that will make you more effective.

Taking Initiative

K.C., a very competent, young Asian engineer with a good command of English, was recently transferred from his home country to the company's headquarters in the U.S. On Monday, his first day on the job, his boss presented him with piles of data related to a problem the business was having. Being very hard working, K.C. set about reading through all of the data and within two days, he had completed that task. Tuesday passed with no further word from his boss as did Wednesday and Thursday. On Friday, his boss appeared and asked K.C. for his report. "Report?" replied K.C., feeling quite confused and embarrassed. K.C. had no report to present.

Taking the next steps without being told

In this situation, the American boss expected that K.C. would not only review all the relevant documents, but would go the next step and, without being asked directly, come up with some proposed solutions to the problem. The American boss assumed that K.C. would take the next step without specifically being directed to do so. K.C. assumed that the boss would clearly tell him to prepare a report with a proposal to solve the business problem, if that was what he wanted. This was a cultural miss which left both parties frustrated.

Working smart, not hard

Americans talk about "working smart, not hard". This means that employees who put in long hours are certainly appreciated, but those who get the job done by taking initiative — looking for new solutions, finding ways of saving time, energy, or money, or going beyond their job description — are valued even more. Thinking ahead, doing more than just what is required and going the next step on your own without having to be told, are characteristics of the manager who gets ahead in American business.

Americans are encouraged from youth to look for creative solutions to problems, to take appropriate risks, to solve problems. As adults, this is expected, even if it's not in one's direct job description. This is valued behavior. Generally, an American boss appreciates employees who can troubleshoot. This means looking ahead to identify possible problems and preventing or addressing them when they are small and easily solvable.

> ### What This Means For You:
>
> To be seen as a doer, be a problem-solver. Anticipate the consequences of any course of action. If you see serious problems, bring them, along with proposed solutions, to the attention of your boss or relevant colleagues.

Volunteering

An Asian group of managers is being trained by an American from the home office in a new management information system. The trainer asks for a volunteer from the group to participate in a role play to demonstrate how to implement the new system. No one volunteers.

Make an impression by being involved

If the American is not familiar with Asian values and behavior, he or she can easily misinterpret this reaction. The trainer may assume either that no one understands the task and/or that the trainees are not willing to cooperate with the training process. In either case, the American trainer would have misread the participants' reactions and is likely to end up confused, frustrated, and possibly angry. The trainer expects trainees to volunteer. Volunteering, answering questions, offering opinions all show initiative in a training situation, from an American point of view.

For many Asians, this type of behavior, either in a training situation or in a business meeting, can be uncomfortable. In general, Americans are much less concerned about making a mistake or about how others in the group view them. They have been taught from early years that it is appropriate to volunteer their thoughts in group discussions. They have learned that this behavior is expected and that it is one way to let their superiors know that they are involved, interested, and able. Showing that you are involved through thoughtful participation in the discussion is an American way of making a good impression in a business meeting.

Talking about Problems

Mr. Sutheevitanunt from the Bangkok office of an American multinational was at company headquarters in New York for a review of the directions the company was going to take in Thailand. As the only Asian at the meeting, he was reserved as others generated ideas and formulated the company's plans. Just before the meeting was about to break up, Mr. Sutheevitanunt, apologetically, offered some comments on why the proposed plans for the future would not work in Thailand. The CEO, quite annoyed, turned to Mr. Sutheevitanunt and said, "Why did you wait so long before presenting this information? We needed this input at the beginning of the meeting, not now!" Mr. Sutheevitanunt felt that the CEO's comment was harsh and insensitive.

Americans want the bad news early

Traditionally in many Asian societies, it has been the job of a good employee to handle problems by himself or herself rather than to bring them to the attention of a superior. Even when this isn't the case, few Asians want to be the bearers of "bad news". This often results in shielding the boss from bad news. In contrast, American managers generally encourage their staff to let them know when problems arise. They want their staff to handle these problems themselves whenever possible, but they also want to be kept informed. They assume that staff will naturally make them aware of any significant problems that come up. In fact, Americans often say, "No news is good news." This means that if they don't hear of any problem, they assume that all is going well. The potential for cross-cultural missing (misunderstanding) is great here. Americans are likely to assume that all is well, unless they hear otherwise, and Asian managers are often reluctant to bring bad news to the attention of the boss. The result is that issues may not get addressed and crises may erupt.

Having a realistic idea of what the problems are gives the American manager a greater sense of control. Being forewarned allows the American manager to come up with an alternative plan to minimize or avoid the damage. American managers hate surprises. They believe that they can effectively deal with almost any situation, if they have enough time, resources, and accurate information with which to plan.

> **What This Means For You:**
>
> *Letting the American manager know about problems early and offering your ideas for solutions increases the American's confidence in you.*

Calling attention to significant obstacles that get in the way of results and suggesting solutions to them is one very concrete way to demonstrate initiative and to build trust with an American manager. While this approach may sound risky to the traditional Asian manager, it is actually less risky than concealing problems from an American manager. Generally speaking, an American wants the bad news early. This gives the manager time to plan an effective response. She or he would prefer to learn from the supervisor of Department A that there is a problem in Department A than to learn of it from someone else or to have it result in a crisis that no one anticipated.

Some Guidelines for Telling Your Boss Bad News

1. **Report the problem as soon as you become aware of it.**
   This allows your supervisor time to address the problem before it gets worse.

2. **Let your boss know, without exaggerating or overstating, that this is an issue that needs attention.**
   Begin by saying something like, "Here is something I think we need to address." Or, "I've come across something I think you need to know about."

3. **Present only the critical facts in the order they occurred.**
   Explain exactly what happened. Rehearse what you are going to say before you meet with your boss.

4. **Have a proposed solution to the problem and be ready to share it, if asked.**
   Focus on specific steps to be taken to correct the error or situation and what can be done in the future to prevent it from happening again. However, if you don't have a solution, it is still important to let your boss know about the problem.

5. **Pass on good news as well as bad news to your boss.**
   This will make the boss more open to hearing your suggestions.

Mistakes

"The one and only serious mistake is to be afraid of making mistakes."

"Mistakes are often the best teachers."

"When life gives you lemons, make lemonade."

— American proverbs

Mistakes are learning opportunities

Perhaps the riskiest area of all for Americans as well as for Asians has to do with admitting mistakes. No one from any culture wants to tell his or her supervisor that they have made a mistake, especially if it's a serious one. Americans, however, often find this somewhat easier to do than Asians, because of the way mistakes are viewed in American culture. In school, Americans learn that, while not desirable, mistakes can be opportunities for learning. In business, Americans expect that inevitably employees will make some mistakes. Again, while not desirable (slogans like, "Do it right the first time," are part of the corporate cultures of many American organizations,) in most cases, neither are they disasters.

In many Asian cultures there is much less room for mistakes. It would be extremely difficult, and perhaps unwise, to admit one's mistakes to a supervisor. Instead, many Asian employees will work extremely hard to correct the mistake, without ever bringing it directly to the boss' attention.

Acting in a traditional Asian fashion in this type of situation with an American supervisor or colleague almost always will cause problems. If the boss finds out that an employee deliberately has concealed a serious mistake (and the chances are quite good that the boss eventually will find out!), the trust between the boss and the employee may well be lost. The American is likely to question what other information has been withheld and his or her confidence in that employee will be badly shaken, if not destroyed.

Americans want to "fix" mistakes

A good American manager, when confronted with an employee's mistake will often ask, "What did you learn from this?" "How can we fix it?" In American culture, a mistake generally is not a cause for dismissal, unless it involves issues of safety, ethics, or breaking the law. What is expected is that the employee learn from his or her mistake and not make the same mistake again. Of course, competence is expected and repeated serious mistakes will be damaging, whether one's boss is American or Asian. Nonetheless, in most cases, it is better when working with an American to admit mistakes rather than to hide them.

What This Means For You:

When it comes to mistakes, it is better to admit them than to hide them. Admitting a mistake and taking steps to fix it or to ensure it will not happen again will generally increase, rather than decrease, an American's trust in you.

Decision-Making

American teachers at an English language institute in an Asian capital city complain about their Director, an Asian with a Ph.D., who makes new policies without consulting the teachers concerned. They do not think the Director respects them because he makes decisions about the curriculum and schedule by himself. On the other hand, the Director thinks the American teachers do not respect him because they regularly question the decisions he makes.

The style of decision-making varies by culture

To make things happen in business, decisions have to be made. Across organizations and across cultures, there are differences in the ways decisions are viewed, the way decisions are made, and how they are implemented. One critical variable seems to be the amount of control held by the boss or supervisor when making a decision. In some cultures, decisions are highly centralized with the authority figure (the boss) responsible for all major, and many seemingly minor, decisions. In other cultures, decision-making is highly decentralized with lower level managers and employees having higher degrees of input and responsibility for many decisions. Perhaps this variation in decision-making is best represented by a continuum with Japan at one end and much of the rest of Asia at the other. America would probably fall somewhere in the middle.

HIGHLY   HIGHLY
DECENTRALIZED   CENTRALIZED

←—————————————————————————→

Japan   America   Thailand,
                                                              Taiwan,
                                                              Malaysia,
                                                              Philippines
                                                              & much of the
                                                              rest of Asia

Japanese   In Japan, the responsibility for corporate success rests
decision-   with all the employees. Japanese business leaders believe
making   that employees should be involved in decisions. Everyone even remotely affected by a decision is consulted. Many ideas or proposals are initiated from lower or middle levels of the organization. Before any action is taken, considerable time is spent defining, evaluating, discussing, and approving or disapproving the issue. Consensus through lengthy discussion, both formal as well as informal, is considered appropriate before a major decision is undertaken. The process takes time. Yet, the decision, once made, can usually be put into effect quickly because all have been involved in the process.

*Other Asian
styles of
decision-
making*

In other Asian societies, the decision-making process may be somewhat different. Business units run like families with the boss taking the role of the father. Like a father, he should consult, involve, and take into account the needs and ideas of his subordinates (his children), but he is the decision-maker. Public explanation, debate, or documentation is not required. The decision-maker does not have to justify his decision openly. He is respected because he has the power and wisdom to make the decisions.

The employee gives input only if asked, but does not expect to be regularly consulted. Traditionally, the subordinate's role is to follow his supervisor's instructions, rather than to make decisions. Once a decision is made, the employee is not to question it, suggest alternatives, or make recommendations. Employees are often reluctant to make decisions, even minor ones, believing that that is the role of their superiors. There is a tendency to put off making decisions by those at lower levels because of fear of loss of face, damage to relationships, or consequences to oneself should the decision be wrong. Little responsibility is delegated downward and responsibility, when things go wrong, is pushed upward.

*Decision-
making,
American-
style*

American managers are trained to make things happen. They admire and promote individuals whom they see as effective decision-makers. Making decisions quickly and logically is seen as a way of getting things done efficiently. Because of their orientation towards taking risks and making mistakes, Americans often will see making a wrong decision as preferable to not making any decision at all. In American culture, people are trained from early childhood to figure out what is best among competing alternatives and, more importantly, to make decisions for and by themselves.

What This Means For You:

You learn to make good decisions through experience. Therefore, you have to push yourself to take the risk and make decisions. American supervisors would prefer that you make decisions and occasionally be wrong, than not make any decisions at all. What is expected of you as a manager in an American company is that you will become an effective decision-maker.

The ideal American manager is first and foremost a good decision-maker. Decisions are made on the basis of logic and accurate information. Therefore, Americans look to gather relevant information (forecasts, market surveys, budgets) as aids to help them make the best decision. Once they have the relevant information, they want to make and implement the decision quickly. Intuition, feelings, or "hunches" are not viewed with the same credibility as facts, statistics, and data.

The consultation model of decision-making

Traditionally, decision-making in American business was "top down", meaning the manager made many decisions without consulting subordinates who might have critical information or perspectives about the issue. Today, this approach is changing. Because Americans generally see consensus as desirable but not necessary or expected, they usually adopt a consultation model, rather than a consensus model, when making decisions. An effective manager is taught to consult with those who can contribute useful information to the topic being considered. As a result, Americans have lots of meetings, committees, and conferences to gather, share, and review relevant information.

In American business, in the last few decades, there has been a trend towards decentralized decision-making. That is, pushing responsibility for decision-making down to those at lower levels within the organization. Increasingly, getting input from all those involved or affected by a decision is seen to be desirable.

Voting

At times, voting is used to make decisions among equals, for example, in a management team, with the majority deciding the course of action. Majority rule decision-making can be uncomfortable for many Asians, as voting draws attention to the minority that was defeated. This can cause embarrassment and disharmony.

Most American staff believe they should have input into decisions which directly affect them. They expect to be able to express their opinions and to have a fair hearing. At the same time, if they have information that is relevant to an important decision being made, they are expected to come forward with it.

What This Means For You:

If an important decision is being made and you have critical information that will affect the success of the decision, share that information with your boss or colleagues, even though it may feel uncomfortable to do so. If it is discovered later that you withheld relevant information, it will be looked upon very unfavorably.

Responsibility for decisions

In an American organization, responsibility for most decisions, big ones as well as small ones, usually can be traced to a specific person. If something goes wrong, American managers expect that person to acknowledge responsibility and not attempt to "pass the buck" (blame the failure on someone else). They are likely to ask, "Who is responsible for this mistake?" They expect the responsible party to take "ownership" for the error or omission. If this doesn't happen, American managers can get quite upset because, in their way of thinking, all problems can be resolved if you address them. If you don't (or can't) address them, they will only get worse or go on forever. In contrast, in many Asian cultures, finding out who is to blame when something goes wrong is not the highest priority. What is important is to repair the damage and to re-establish harmony.

A Decision-Making Strategy that Works with Americans

Making a good decision involves a certain amount of risk. For Americans, the goal is to minimize the risk as much as possible by fully understanding the issue or situation, generating alternatives, choosing the best alternative(s), and making sure the alternative you choose can be implemented.

1. **Be clear on the issue or decision to be made.**
   "What is the real concern?"
   "What is the decision that needs to be made?"
   "What additional information do I need to make this decision?"

2. **Develop options or alternatives.**
   "What are all the possible choices of action in this case?"

3. **Assess the options and compare the alternatives.**
   "What are the advantages of each choice?"
   "What are the disadvantages or risks of each choice?"

4. **Select the best alternative.**
   "Which option maximizes the benefits and minimizes the risks/costs?"
   Remember, not making a decision is itself a decision.

5. **Develop a plan for implementing the decision.**
   "What's my time frame? Who shall I involve? What do I need to do first?"

> 6.   Think through possible obstacles or blocks.
>   *"What can go wrong? How can I prevent it?"*
>
> 7.   Implement the plan with scheduled evaluation(s).

Delegating

Delegating, American-style

Delegating is giving subordinates the opportunity to do the job that their bosses would usually do. As a general rule, Americans value delegating. American managers are encouraged to give responsibility and decision-making authority for carrying out specific activities to subordinates at all levels of an organization. It is a natural outgrowth of the values of individuality, equality, and independence.

In general, effective American managers believe that delegating provides a way for them to multiply their time, energy, and ability, to take on many projects and get a lot done, through the input and involvement of others. They believe the people directly involved should make the relevant decisions and take responsibility for a task or project. They should personally be rewarded for the success of the project and held accountable for its failure. This, they believe, promotes ownership and initiative.

What This Means For You:

With an American boss, ask to take on projects or assignments. This is a chance for you to demonstrate your talents and abilities. Remember, however, by taking on a task you also assume responsibility for its completion and its success or failure.

Americans may misinterpret Asian modesty

Because of the cultural differences relating to self-reliance, independence, and modesty, American managers often misunderstand the reaction of Asian staff to tasks that are delegated. When assigned a task, Asian staff often play down their competence. For example, there is a tendency among Malaysians (and other Asians) to respond with such statements as, "I'm not sure I can do it, but I will try." Or, "I have finished the project, but I don't know if I have done it correctly," (Abdullah, 1992). While the Asian may be saving face and not wanting to appear overly confident or self-assured, the American may interpret this behavior as reflecting a lack of self-confidence and may question the competence of the Asian manager. The American manager may think, "If he doesn't think he can do a good job, then he probably won't."

Meetings

Pak Bambang has been with an American firm in Jakarta for over a year and regularly attends the weekly staff meetings. He continues to be amazed that the meetings move so briskly and that decisions seem to be made abruptly, without what he would consider a full airing. He senses that there are other Indonesian managers at the meeting who don't always agree with the actions being taken, yet they don't object. Moving things along, rather than spending time on collective review and consideration, seems to be the purpose of American staff meetings.

Meetings are for sharing information

American companies hold many meetings. Coming from an individual-centered society, Americans have to put energy into working together. For Asians, working with and through other people generally comes more easily. This is part of the necessary skills one learns growing up in a group-based culture. American companies hold meetings, first and foremost, to share information. Unlike the traditional Asian business, where significant information is known and shared by the key players, in an American company information tends to be compartmentalized and generally not shared, except formally (i.e. memos, timelines, workplans, budgets). Therefore, meetings are important as a formal way to share information. Usually, the purpose of a meeting in American business is not to give formal approval or to get consensus on decisions that have already been made. Rather, in addition to sharing information, meetings are used to generate ideas or solutions to problems, get input on decisions, help people from different departments work together, and bring staff together to develop a sense of team or group unity.

What This Means For You:

Think through agenda items carefully before a meeting. Bring appropriate facts and figures with you to the meeting to support your position(s). If you are making a presentation or expected to address or respond to an agenda item, practice actually presenting your ideas or report beforehand. (Rehearse, saying what you are going to say in front of a mirror or with a friend.) Have a summary of major points for yourself, and, if appropriate, an information handout for other participants.

Meetings are for getting things done

Americans want leadership that keeps meetings "on track" (focused) and brief. They want the meeting to have a clear purpose and to end with an agreement or action plan. They object to meetings that are too long or not focused on important issues. They expect everyone attending a meeting to share a common commitment to exchange information, to achieve results, to present his or her views energetically, and to reach decisions on critical agenda issues even if some participants may not be entirely satisfied with the result. They want a meeting to achieve something and not waste their time. They expect there will be differences of opinion and that airing these differences ultimately will result in the best outcome.

Running an Effective Meeting American-Style

Before the Meeting:

1. *Define the objective(s) of the meeting.*
   Be clear about what you want to accomplish. Focus on issues that you and other members of the group see as relevant. Get input from other participants.

2. *Prepare an agenda.*
   Place the most urgent issues at the top of the agenda.

3. *Give out the agenda before the meeting.*

At the Meeting:

1. *Begin on time.*

2. *Review the agenda and determine priorities.*
   Allowing input on new items and changing priorities foster the participant's commitment to address issues.

3. *Follow the agenda.*
   Defer new issues brought up to the "new business" part of the meeting, another future meeting, or sub-committee. Bring people who stray from the agenda back to agreed-upon issues.

4.   *Make action plans.*
For each decision made, determine who is responsible for implementing it and set target dates for task accomplishment.

5.   *Review agreements reached and decisions made before closing the meeting.*

6.   *End the meeting at or before the scheduled time.*

7.   *Keep a written record (minutes) of decisions made, action taken, concerns raised.*

After the Meeting:

1.   *Distribute the minutes or summary of the meeting to participants as soon as possible after the meeting.*

2.   *Follow-up to assure that tasks assigned are progressing satisfactorily.*
Remind participants of their commitments, encourage them to complete tasks assigned, and acknowledge tasks completed.

3.   *Add any agenda items that have not been addressed to the agenda for the next meeting.*

(Milstein, 1983)

The Good Boss

You have an employee of long standing with the company. He is having serious personal problems which are interfering with his performance on the job. What would you do?

The "ideal" Asian boss

Most traditional Asian business organizations are like a large family, where the boss is like a father. In Indonesia, in fact, the boss is frequently called *bapak* (father). Junior female employees in a Chinese company are often referred to as *xiao jie* (little sister). While much of this traditional style of organizing is changing in Asian business today, there is much that remains the same.

Traditionally, the ideal boss plays a role similar to that of a caring and nurturing parent, offering protection and an on-going commitment to his employees (sons and daughters) in exchange for loyalty and hard work. The famous Chinese saying, "Those who care for others are forever cared for; those who respect others are forever respected," points out the critical characteristics of a good boss.

The ideal boss is competent in running the business, but he is also sensitive and understanding. He works hard to maintain harmony among the employees (in the family). He has a concern for the overall welfare of his staff, not just the issues that relate to productivity at work. Getting an employee's child into university, being concerned about a subordinate's sick parent, attending important ceremonies such as weddings and funerals, are all legitimate concerns and opportunities for involvement for a traditional Asian boss. He is able to maintain a relationship of trust and understanding with subordinates, always remaining calm, pleasant, and polite.

The traditional Asian boss has a status that demands that subordinates defer to him, recognize his position, authority and wisdom, and show that respect through a variety of formal and informal ways. He wants to know all that is going on in the company and requires that all decisions, even relatively minor ones, pass through him. He is sensitive to problems before they are openly presented and works hard to prevent them from surfacing and disrupting morale or the effective functioning of the organization. He also makes the hard decisions, when necessary, and takes responsibility for the failures of his subordinates.

The "ideal" American boss

The definition of the ideal American boss is quite different. Given the segmented nature of American life, the relationship between an employee and a supervisor is essentially a business one and is not likely to go beyond working hours. The American boss is typically reluctant to get involved in the personal life of colleagues or subordinates.

The ideal American boss, who may be a man or a woman, is first and foremost a person who gets things done, both on his own and by motivating and helping others to do the same. To do this, he must be able to work well with people. He believes in delegating, letting those below him make decisions and take responsibility for specific projects or tasks. He values and is valued for future planning and future problem prevention. He is rewarded for making effective and timely decisions based upon quantifiable variables (information you can measure). He prides himself on being able to deal with issues and problems as they come up.

In relating to subordinates, the ideal American boss these days is a coach — motivating, counseling, and problem-solving with members of the team to achieve a common goal. He aims to work with employees to provide interesting, challenging work and career development opportunities. He strives to be fair and not show favoritism to one employee over another. He works towards establishing good team or department morale for he believes that a pleasant, cooperative work environment is a productive one. However, if pushed to decide between getting the job done and the personal feelings or needs of an employee, he ordinarily will chose the former, even at the expense of dismissing underperforming employees.

The Good Employee

Mr. Costello is a senior computer programmer for a Japanese company in America. One day, his supervisor, Mr. Nakamura, calls him in to his office and tells him of a career opportunity with the company in Latin America. Because of his specialized skills, Mr. Costello would be put in charge of developing a new softwear system for a large project the company just won. This would mean three to four years away from the U.S., but a significant overseas bonus plus expanded career opportunities for the future. Mr. Costello thanks Mr. Nakamura for offering him this opportunity but states that before he can commit, he must confer with his wife, a lawyer who recently got her degree. Two days later, Mr. Costello informs Mr. Nakamura that he will not be accepting the offer because he feels it is the wrong time to make an international transfer. His wife is just getting established in a professional career and they have two adolescent children in high school. Mr. Nakamura says nothing but is surprised that Mr. Costello places personal and family considerations over performing a needed and valuable service to the company.

The "ideal" Asian employee

While changing in the last few decades because of greater mobility, urbanization, and the explosion of opportunities for talented managers, loyalty to the company and to one's supervisor remains a cornerstone of the definition of a valued employee throughout Asia. Loyalty, hard work, and the ability to work as a member of a group have traditionally been, and to this day are, among the important characteristics of the ideal employee in Asia. Staying within your job description, not complaining, and following the leadership of your superiors, are all hallmarks of a good worker. The good manager is sensitive and responsive to the wishes and orders of his superior . He does not challenge or disagree with his superior, nor does he offer suggestions unless he is specifically asked. He shields the boss from bad news, fixing problems when he can, diverting them when he can't. When decisions are required, they either are made by concensus, which is the case in Japan, or passed upward to the boss for a decision, which is the case in much of the rest of Asia.

The "ideal" American employee

Americans, on the other hand, have a very different definition of what makes an effective employee or manager. Americans, like Asians, typically desire staff who are loyal and steady. More than that, Americans want employees who "work smart, not hard." This does not mean that Americans do not value hard work.

Rather, it means that working hard will not be valued as highly as working smart. To an American, working smart means figuring out ways to get the job done more efficiently and productively.

Staff who are result-oriented, who look ahead, and who consistently look for ways to improve systems or productivity are frequently more highly valued than those who simply work hard. Such staff generally require limited supervision and are focused on the "big picture", not just their piece of the project or their department. Americans admire (and promote) managers who can assess a situation quickly, who recommend and follow-through with solutions to problems, who are able to work well with others both within and outside of their team, and who have strong analytical and communication skills.

8

The Change-Oriented American

Cultures in Contrast: Change vs. Tradition

Mr Torres, a Filipino manager with an American multinational company in Manila, heaves a sigh. Mr. Anderson, his third American boss in four years, has been on the job for just a month. In that time, he has re-arranged the office furniture, hired a new personal secretary, introduced a new reporting system, and is now considering changes to the company's marketing approach. Mr. Torres wonders why Mr. Anderson is so dissatisfied with everything.

For Asians, the past is the guide to the future

Historically, Asians have looked to the past as a guide for how to proceed in the future. It is not difficult to convince an Asian young person that history is important. Asians are aware of their history. They usually love history and do not need to be told that the past is important. The average Asian, educated or not, has a huge storehouse of knowledge — folk stories and legends, knowledge of important people and events from the past. The past, more than anything else, defines who they are, be they Vietnamese, Indonesian, or Korean. One famous Malay proverb, "Better that the child should perish rather than tradition," can still be heard on the streets of Kuala Lumpur today. It reflects the importance Asian cultures have placed on links to the past.

Traditionally, what has worked in the past has been seen as the safest and most reasonable way to proceed in the future. In many Asian societies, the distant past is remembered as a golden age in which people lived simply and peacefully with each other. There was little conflict and there were enough material goods for all. The world is seen as having gotten worse, not better, since that time. If you look at the editorial page of many Asian newspapers, articles that begin with, "In the past . . ." or "Formerly, . . ." generally follow with a discussion of something positive. When articles begin with "Currently, . . . " or "In modern times, . . ." what generally follows is something negative.

Asian cultures are cultures with long histories. They have a tremendous amount of stability, a great amount of conservatism. Beneath the surface today, all kinds of traditional patterns and beliefs continue to go on. Thai tycoons consult astrologers to determine the best day to buy a company or to sell shares on the stock market. Japanese industrialists, when faced with a rash of accidents in a plant, will bring in a Shinto priest to bless the plant and protect it against evil spirits. Chinese managers, throughout Asia, will consult with *feng-shui* experts to determine the most appropriate site for their buildings, offices, and homes. Malay factory owners will consult with a *bomoh* (traditional healer) when mass hysteria breaks out among assembly line workers.

Change can be dangerous

Traditionally, change has been seen as dangerous in Asian cultures, more likely to bring about trouble than positive benefits. We need to go back to the small village out of which so many Asian values came to see where this belief had its origins. When life is on the edge and survival is at stake, one uses what has worked in the past. To experiment with the rice crop, for instance, would be foolish. If your experiment fails, your family starves. In this respect, it is better to follow what you know will work i.e. a system tested over hundreds of years. The net result is that in the past Asian cultures pushed people in the direction of being cautious, more comfortable with the way things were traditionally done. While this is certainly changing in today's vibrant Asian economies, the cultural tradition is for managers to take their cues from what has worked before, what is customary and predictable.

If Asians dislike change, what explains Asia's incredible economic growth?

How, then, can we explain the tremendous amount of change and innovation that has occurred in Asian societies over the last few decades? How can we account for the economic success of Japan, the four dragons, and the quickly developing economies of China, Indonesia, Malaysia, Thailand, and Vietnam? This seems to contradict all that we have said about traditional Asian conservatism. A factor which is critical in explaining these dramatic changes is the Asian cultural value of pragmatism.

Pragmatism means coping with reality as you find it. Historically, environmental conditions were difficult for many in Asian cultures, particularly East Asian cultures. Being pragmatic or practical when it came to survival issues was essential. You needed to be responsive to the world around you and change to accommodate it. If you did not, you and your family would not survive. The Asian entrepreneur carried these lessons with him from the farm to the marketplace. He learned to be open to change when it would bring direct and obvious economic or survival benefits. Once Asian businesspeople understand the need for change and its potential benefits, they can be very effective and quick in making the change. If the change is of a theoretical or procedural nature, or not obviously to their benefit, Asians may be more resistant to change, preferring the customary or known ways of doing things, even if these procedures may not be, from an American perspective, the most effective or efficient.

Americans view change positively

For most Americans, change is viewed quite differently. In American history, change generally led to positive things, even when the change was painful at the time. The people who settled America, whether from Europe or from Asia, were risk-takers. They left behind what was known and secure and ventured into a new land to make their fortunes. They risked everything in their move to America.

Once in America, the new settlers discovered that, with the increasing economic opportunities of a new, rich land, risks more often resulted in gains than in losses. Even if you tried something and failed, it was possible to pick yourself up and try again. The opportunities were there and they were plentiful. Chinese immigrants arriving on the West coast more than a hundred years ago referred to their port of entry, San Francisco, as the "golden mountain". Traditionally for Americans, there has been a strong belief that the future holds promise, that economic conditions are ever-improving and that one's children will live better than oneself. (In recent years, this view has been challenged by the economic realities of low growth and high unemployment.)

American politicians regularly campaign on the issue, "It is time for change." On a personal level, Americans seem to thrive on change. They view change, in and of itself, as a positive goal. They will often say, "I need a change," if they have been with a job or task too long. They have become accustomed, in the fast-paced U.S., to high levels of stimulation (change) and if they don't get enough of it, they may feel dissatisfied or bored. A survey on American managers revealed that one out of every two American office workers had changed employers in the past five years and that at any one time three out of ten managers are circulating their résumés in search of a better job, even when their job is secure (Feinsibler & Mead, 1980).

Emphasis upon youth

Related to the issue of change is how age and seniority are viewed. Elders in Asian society are honored, respected, and their advice heeded. They are the conveyors of the wisdom of the past. In American society, a lot of value is placed on youth. Youth is associated with vigor, with enthusiasm, and with energy.

Hundreds of millions of dollars are spent each year in America on face lifts, hair transplants, wrinkle cream, and hair dyes, all designed to maintain the image of youthfulness. Sadly, the wisdom and experience of older Americans is often not appreciated or sought after, as the focus is on the new, the young and the modern. One way this may be reflected at work is when an American supervisor who holds an M.B.A. from a prestigious university may be younger and less experienced than those whom he or she supervises.

Business Applications

Change as Opportunity

Americans believe change leads to progress

For most American managers, introducing change, especially change meant to improve business opportunities, increase efficiency or improve productivity is seen as the logical way to approach a business problem. Efforts should be made to find new and better ways to do things. It is also the way to be noticed by upper management, to "make your mark", to get ahead. Sometimes, according to many non-American businesspeople, American companies seem to embrace change just for the sake of change. American managers have been accused of adopting new business concepts or strategies almost in a faddish manner — one year it is Management By Objectives (MBO) and the next year it is Total Quality Management (TQM). This can be difficult on the manager who prefers continuity and stability.

> **What This Means For You:**
>
> *When working for an American company, you can expect frequent reviews and changes in procedures. Likewise, when you get a new American boss, she or he often will look for ways to "improve" on the way things are done. Expect new American supervisors to make changes. That is their way of making the new position their own.*

Mr. Wu, the proud manager of the most productive plant in his new American company, received a memo from the Vice-President saying that all plant managers were required to attend a five-day training program "to improve management skills and reach full potential". Glancing up at the productivity awards mounted on his wall,

Mr. Wu cannot understand what he has done wrong and why his skills need improvement.

Self-improvement

Americans tend to believe that almost anything can be made better. This includes themselves. The American belief in self-improvement is reflected in the many self-help books which can be found in any American bookstore. These give advice on how to be more successful and happy by improving everything from your golf games, to your public speaking skills to your marriage.

The number of training opportunities in the typical American organization reflect this belief that people can and should continue to learn and improve. By regularly reading professional literature and attending training programs, the American believes he or she can become more effective on the job.

Taking Risks

A position became open on the senior management team in an American company's Seoul office. The Korean staff fully expected that Mr. Park would be named to the position. After all, he was the most senior Korean on staff and had served the company loyally for the last fifteen years. They were shocked when instead, Mr. Rhee, who had only been with the company for three years, was named to the position. What caught the eye of senior management in the home office was Mr. Rhee's recent suggestions for revamping the company's marketing strategy. This was the kind of bold approach they were looking for.

Change is, by its very nature, risky. When you try something new, something different, you can never be sure how it will turn out. It is possible that loss or harm could come from making a change or from putting yourself in a new situation. Alternatively, change creates the possibility for good things to happen. How you look at risk is very much affected by your cultural background.

Americans have been rewarded for taking risks

Historically, Americans have been more comfortable in taking risks than most Asians. Risk takers frequently have been rewarded in American society, be they explorers, pioneers, investors, or entrepreneurs. Americans say to each other, "Nothing ventured, nothing gained." This means you have to take a risk in order to succeed. In American culture, taking risks, whether in business or in your personal life, is seen as necessary for gain or growth. You see this belief reflected in the high number of new business start-ups each year and the number of managers willing to leave secure jobs for "greener pastures" (better jobs).

Entrepreneurs in both Asian and American cultures traditionally have been willing to take risks to become successful. Differences between Asians and Americans in business with regard to risk taking are more significant lower down in the organization, for example, at the level of managers and other employees.

In American business, managers are rewarded for taking initiative, making decisions, and identifying and solving problems. All of these behaviors involve a willingness to make judgements and to take risks. American managers are expected to treat risks much as they do any other business problem. They are expected to evaluate risks carefully, weighing pros, cons and probabilities. They are expected to anticipate potential problems with each course of action. Americans believe you can reduce risk by having a clear definition of the goal, task, or project and by identifying and addressing the risk factors. Because of their cultural tradition with risk-taking, Americans may be more likely than many of their Asian counterparts to go for "home runs" — taking bigger risks so they can gain bigger rewards.

Given their sense of individualism, their desire to be noticed, to achieve, and to make a difference, ambitious American managers are looking for ways to stand out. By finding ways to excel and be noticed, American managers improve their changes of getting promoted.

Having the judgement and the ability to take appropriate risks often separates managers who will get ahead from those who will not in American business.

For Asians, taking risks is risky

Traditionally, in Asia, there have been few rewards or incentives for Asian managers to take the same types of risks that are expected of American managers. For the traditional Asian employee, the surest route to advancement was to do his job well and not go beyond what was expected. Traditionally, making decisions and accepting the risks attached to them, were the job of the boss. As an employee, to take risks and to try new things in a business environment that emphasized tradition, consistency, and stability, were, in themselves, very risky activities. Such activities could lead to disastrous consequences if they failed and only limited gain for the individual, if they succeeded.

As economic opportunities have expanded in Asia, Asian managers have grown more comfortable at taking risks. There has been a shift from basic industries that have copied designs originating in the West to high tech, creative enterprises that require significant corporate and managerial risk-taking. Nevertheless, Asian managers, in general, are more cautious and less willing to take risks than their American corporate colleagues. They may require a likelihood of success and more support from their colleagues and superiors before they try something new and different.

What This Means For You:

To get ahead in an American company, you need to be seen as someone who takes "appropriate" risks, after carefully weighing and considering the options.

Time Management

"The early bird catches the worm."

"Don't put off until tomorrow what you can do today."

"There is a time and place for everything."

— *American proverbs*

Different views of time

"Of course I need it today. If I needed it tomorrow, I would ask for it tomorrow," is something an American boss might say, half jokingly, to a subordinate. American impatience with time is legendary. Certainly, Asian businesspeople living and working in Asia's fast-paced urban centers have an appreciation of the importance of time. Yet, there seems to be a difference in how Americans and Asians relate to time and time commitments.

Traditional rural Asian societies looked at time in broad sweeps. Time was viewed as a series of recurring cycles — the planting season, the monsoon season, the harvesting season, with one cycle following the next. People of traditional Asian cultures got up at dawn and worked in the fields until the work was done, be it five hours or ten hours, depending on the stage in the rice growing cycle. Eating, sleeping, working, and socializing were activities which flowed, one from the other, without clear distinctions. Time is not nearly as scarce a resource in a rural fishing or farming village as it is in an urban industrial city.

The American perspective on time developed out of the experience of becoming an industrialized country. This transition from agriculture to industry happened over 100 years ago. This means that Americans have a much longer history of dealing with time as a scarce commodity. With the exception of Japan which became industrialized much earlier, many of the societies of Asia made the transition from agriculture to industry within the last few decades. Others still have a strong agricultural component.

Most Asian businesspeople over the age of thirty grew up in societies that were largely agricultural in nature, where a different, more relaxed, attitude towards time prevailed. Attitudes about time with which you are raised tend to persist, to some degree, in your adult life. Modern industrial society has required that both Asians and Americans alike pay much greater attention to time. While Asian and American managers, to a great extent, have converged on how they see and use time, significant cultural differences still separate the two.

To an American, time is scarce

To the average American, time is a very scarce commodity. Americans never seem to have enough of it. American English is filled with phrases that indicate how real and important time is to Americans. They talk about "spending time", "losing time", "saving time", and definitely not wanting to "waste time". Using your time wisely and efficiently so that you can get more done is the theme of hundreds of books on time management. Getting things done "on time" is a high priority in American business. This emphasis on time, arising originally out of the requirements of the industrial revolution, is one of the reasons why the American economy has been so productive.

> **What This Means For You:**
>
> *Since Americans may be "booked up" in their appointment calendar far in advance, it is important to request appointments with plenty of advance notice, if possible.*

An effective manager uses time wisely

To Americans, time is like a straight line with a definite beginning and definite end point. They act as if a day is only present for a brief moment and the next day is nearly here. Americans say that "time marches on", meaning you have only a limited amount of this precious commodity and you should use it wisely and efficiently.

Effective managers are in control of their time. They dedicate their time to high priority tasks. This orientation to the clock gives an urgency, an emotional push, to time for Americans that many Asians may not feel to the same degree.

An American will arrive for an appointment and, after a few minutes of casual conversation, say, "Let me get right to the point. The reason I'm here today is . . . " From the American perspective, this is efficient but also polite because it communicates a respect for the host's time. To many Asians, this can feel rude, calculating, or somehow out of order. They may ask, "How can you do business before you warm up the relationship?"

Americans are always in a hurry

Americans always seem to be fighting the battle of the clock and losing. They are aware of the clock ticking away, of time running out. One American in four reports always feeling rushed (Feinsilber et al, 1980). There never seems to be enough time in the day to accomplish all the tasks on the "to do" list. People are always hurrying, cramming as much as possible into each day. Americans at work often convey a sense of urgency about projects and deadlines. While Thais may say *mai pen rai* and Malays may say *tidak apa* (never mind — it's not so important), Americans will say, "It must be done now. It must be done on time."

An American manager might say to an Asian colleague with whom he or she is negotiating, "Your boss will have to make up his mind soon because my Board meets next week and I have to have an answer by then." To the Asian executive, this request may seem rude and overdemanding, exerting undue pressure in a situation over which he may not have control. What "urgent" may mean in American culture, and the importance that is attached to it, may be very different than what that very same word may mean in the Filipino, Chinese, or Indonesian culture.

Time is used like a ruler — one task at a time

The average American uses time like a ruler. It is divided into pieces, marked off, and scheduled. Generally, Americans believe it is most productive to pay attention to one task at a time. Jobs, projects or meetings, like appointments in a diary, are scheduled and compartmentalized. When they finish one project, they then go on to the next one. They believe this is the most efficient way to use their time. This contrasts with the approach of people from numbers of Asian (and other) cultures who are used to being involved with many things at once. This is why Americans don't like to be interrupted if they are in the middle of a task or project. This is why they believe agendas for meetings are so critical. (Agendas keep you on track in a logical, scheduled order.) This is why private offices and one-on-one meetings with staff to address specific, clearly defined issues are so important. (You can deal with one person, on one issue, at one time.)

What This Means For You:

If you want to interrupt an American at work, ask:
> *"When would be a good time to talk about . . . ?" or*
> *"Is this a good time to talk about . . . ?"*

Time commitments are taken seriously

Time commitments are taken very seriously by most Americans. Americans say, "Time is money." To be called "efficient" is high praise for an American manager. In an American company, you are evaluated not only on how well you get the job done, but how fast you do it.

Being on time (punctual) is important in America, as it is in many parts of Asia. Businesspeople in America consider it rude if you are late to a meeting, especially if you are the junior colleague. They normally try to arrive five minutes before the scheduled meeting time.

What This Means For You:

If you know you will be late for a meeting with an American, call and inform your colleague that you will be late and when you expect to arrive. If an American is coming to your office and you must keep him or her waiting, apologize and let the American know approximately how much longer it will be before you will be free.

Tips on Time Management

In order to be as efficient and productive as possible during the time you have each day in the office:

1. **Plan your time.**
   Organize your day and week by making lists of "things to do" for the following day or week. Have a plan and start each day with a set of goals to accomplish.

2. **Plan for interruption.**
   Give yourself more time for tasks than you think you will need.

3. **Prioritize.**
    Focus on the important tasks. Eliminate the unimportant. Try to accomplish one major objective each day.

4. **Delegate.**
    Examine which of your tasks can be assigned to subordinates. Don't get overwhelmed in details.

5. **Schedule appointments with yourself.**
    For big projects that need uninterrupted time for you to think, research, and write, mark off time on your calendar just like any other meeting.

6. **Schedule your "prime time" for your most important tasks.**
    Prime time is the period of the day when you are most effective, have the most energy, and are best able to concentrate.

7. **Fight procrastination.**
    Procrastination means putting off until tomorrow things that should be done today. Set deadlines for yourself and keep to them. At the beginning of each day (or week), do the hardest task first. By so doing, you would have gotten it out of the way.

Planning, Schedules, and Timelines

Planning is important

Americans have traditionally believed that what happens in the future is, to a great degree, within their control. They believe they can make change happen. They say, "Where there is a will (the desire), there is a way (to make a change happen)." The American manager believes that planning for the future is an important way of controlling the future. You can make a difference, if you go about it in the right way. The result is that in American business a lot of time, resources, and attention are given to the planning process. That is how Americans have been taught to make change happen.

While many American managers welcome change, they do not like surprises. They dislike being caught off balance by a sudden announcement or development. Knowing a change in advance gives them a chance to think about and plan for it.

What This Means For You:

If you know a change is coming, be sure your American boss or colleague isn't the last to know.

Plans are made based on objective data

When Americans plan, they look to data, numbers, and probabilities to help them make the best plan or decision. They are suspicious of judgements which are not based on concrete, observable, or measurable data. They believe you can quantify or measure almost anything — be it work output, market potential, or employee performance. Success or failure is measured in statistics or numbers. This primarily quantitative approach can be frustrating to Asian managers who often plan and make decisions based upon qualitative as well as quantitative data — information you can measure as well as information that is intuitive or which "feels right".

Ms. Leung is frequently given what she sees as unrealistic timelines for completing projects assigned her by her American boss. By working late, coming in weekends, and enlisting the help of her colleagues, she manages to complete these projects on time. Her American boss is pleased and often comments to other Americans about the top-notch efficiency of her Singaporean staff. She is taken completely by surprise when Ms. Leung submits her resignation, citing family obligations as the reason for leaving. In reality,

Ms. Leung has decided to seek employment elsewhere. She hopes to find a boss who will be more considerate of the staff and more realistic about the time it takes to get the job done.

Timelines and deadlines

For the typical American businessperson, schedules, timelines, and deadlines give a sense of order, control, and predictability to any task. Americans generally like to end meetings with a plan, a path forward, or next steps to be undertaken. If a plan doesn't work or conditions change, they want to re-evaluate the workplan or timeline and make another, more realistic, one.

Missing deadlines or being off on a timeline affects American managers differently than their Asian colleagues. For many Asians, at least traditionally, a schedule or deadline is a goal to try to meet in a world which has many variables outside of your control. Since you can't control all the variables (other peoples' reactions, unforeseen delays, the economic climate, etc.), Asians have traditionally viewed a deadline or schedule as an intention or best estimate of what you will be able to achieve.

For Americans, starting with the very different assumption that they, to a great extent, can control their world, schedules, timelines, or deadlines seem to take on a life of their own. Timelines, schedules, and lists of things "to do" increase a task's importance and create a sense of urgency. Americans are very serious about deadlines. Their value is unquestionable. Without deadlines, American managers believe, few jobs would get done on time. Control and predictability would be lost and business, as they know it, would come to a halt. It is no wonder, then, that American managers can get extremely distressed if deadlines are missed.

American managers believe that if subordinates see that they will not be able to meet a timeline with a reasonable amount of effort, it is the subordinate's responsibility to discuss this issue with his or her supervisor. The best time to do this is right at the beginning, when timelines are first established. Even after the project or task is underway, timelines can sometimes be renegotiated. The solution may be adding more staff to get the job done or relieving staff of other responsibilities, so they can focus on the priority assignment and meet the deadline. In any case, problem solving will be applied to regain control of the situation. Asians, like Ms. Leung, may be reluctant to bring this type of issue up with their supervisor. They may think it is not their role to question a supervisor's decisions or to say they cannot meet an expectation.

> **What This Means For You:**
>
> *As soon as you realize that you can't meet a deadline or keep to a timeline, inform your supervisor so that you can either renegotiate the time frames or get more resources to allow you to get the job done on schedule.*

Future Orientation

Americans look to the future

Most Americans do not share the typical Asian's affection for the past. In part, this is because their historical past consists of only a few hundred years and because they are a nation of immigrants, each with a different past which they left behind in the "old country". Americans believe one should look towards the future and not dwell on the past. For Americans, an openness to change, to shed the past, has frequently resulted in increased opportunities and a better life. Rather than looking back to the past for a sense of direction, Americans tend to look forward, to the future. The past and its traditions have little hold over most Americans, especially when making decisions about current day to day matters.

New is better

Americans love things that are new and different. They are always inventing new products and improving on old ones. If you review American advertisements in newspapers, magazines, or on television, you will note that words such as "new" and "improved" are often used.

American managers typically care about and focus on the experience of the previous year or two. They speak about beating the previous year's results and they usually carry forward key learnings only from that year. The experience of the previous number of years may be interesting, but it is somewhat irrelevant when coming up with solutions to problems faced today.

Control +
change =
progress

The majority of Americans believe they can shape their own future. Their experience in building a nation has convinced them that their physical and social surroundings can be dominated or controlled by human effort. Progress, a better future, is not only possible, but within their grasp and something they should work hard to achieve.

In general, Americans believe that through controlled change, they can improve the human condition and they can do it immediately. They talk about "defeating AIDS", "eradicating poverty", and "conquering space". This value of working to make tomorrow better is reflected in the slogans and mission statements of many American companies, e.g. "Progress is our middle name," "Progress is our most important product," "Better living for tomorrow." American managers are impatient with, and do not respect, colleagues they see as passively accepting poor or substandard business performance. They believe you can always improve.

What This Means For You:

To get ahead in an American company, focus on how things can be made better, what steps can be taken to improve sales or production figures, how processes can be made more cost-efficient.

The American manager gets sent on a business trip to Asia to scout out sales possibilities. His boss says, "You'd better bring back some business. This trip is costing the company $10,000." A Japanese executive comes to America for the same reason. His boss says, "Learn what you can about the market and the people. Begin to develop relationships. We're in no hurry to make a decision. We want to be sure it is the right decision."

Short-term future perspective

Although Americans tend to focus on the future, their focus tends to be on the short-term future. Americans want things to happen fast. They want to see the immediate results of their efforts. Culturally, Americans have a reputation of being "sprinters" — short distance runners who have great bursts of energy and drive in the short run, but who tire in the longer distances. Americans in business have great drive and determination in the immediate future, but often have difficulty, when compared with many of their Asian counterparts, in maintaining that energy and commitment long-term, unless there are visible rewards for their efforts.

To an American in business, long-term may be five to seven years down the road. This arises, at least in part, from the way American business is structured, with shareholders concerned about earning dividends. This forces American executives to pay attention to the next quarter's results, often at the expense of longer-term goals. In addition, the amount of change that normally occurs in an American company means that it is hard to comfortably project or plan more than a few years into the future.

This short-term perspective tends to impact on almost every aspect of American business — from marketing to customer relations, from finance to employee relations. For example, the Japanese manager going overseas expects to be posted in the foreign country for six to eight years. He has time to learn the local language, cultivate business contacts, and become familiar with how to work within the specific cultural and business conditions of the location. His supervisor in Osaka knows international business takes time and doesn't expect miracles overnight.

The American transferee, on the other hand, may be assigned abroad for two years or less, is faced with demands for productivity immediately upon arrival, and must respond to a boss who is concerned about stockholders reactions to the next quarter's earnings. Staff in the home office in Chicago, for example, may not understand why it is taking so much longer than expected for objectives to be accomplished or changes to be made. They may not see why the short-term solution may not be the most effective or successful approach. Although this perspective does not seem to be to their advantage in many places around the world, it is the reality of the way many American businesses operate today. It is something American business leaders recognize and which many are attempting to change.

What This Means For You:

Encourage visits from decision-makers in the home office. Acquaint them with the cultural realities of the on-site situation and encourage them to develop a long-term strategy for business success in Asia.

9

The "Follow the Rules" American

Cultures in Contrast: Shame vs. Guilt

An American mother may say to her two-year old son who is misbehaving in public, "Don't act like that. Good boys should behave in public." The Asian mother, equally concerned, might say something like, "Don't act like that. People will say you are a naughty boy. What will they think of our family?" The American mother appeals to a set of rules or standards that her youngster should follow. The Asian mother appeals to the embarrassment that might come to the family from the youngster's poor public behavior.

People who study cultures around the world note that there are two different ways societies attempt to control behavior. They have been labeled "shame" and "guilt". Every society uses both psychological techniques to get people to follow rules which allow them to live, work, and interact harmoniously with others. Those cultures with a group-based orientation favor shame as the main way to control the way people behave. Those societies with an individual-based orientation (Canada, the U.S.A., Europe) tend to rely more on guilt as the main means of control.

Shame: The desire to not be embarrassed publicly

In a group-based culture, you always are seen as a representative of your group (family, company, school). If you do good deeds and are well-received by others, your group gains face, i.e. status, prestige, and honor. If you do things that go against society's rules, not only you, but your entire group, suffers a loss of face. Because the power of the group is so strong, and individuals are so connected to the groups to which they belong, people in shame-based cultures go out of their way to not do things that will bring social disapproval to themselves or to their group. Public shame is something to be avoided at all costs. Fear of public shame, humiliation, or embarrassment — losing face — becomes a strong motivator that discourages people from breaking society's rules.

Guilt: When you feel bad for having done something wrong

In an individual-based culture, where the power of groups is less strong, a different model of social control evolved. Western societies developed the idea that there are certain God-given and societal laws that everyone should follow. This idea has it roots in Judaism and Christianity and was reinforced by the Industrial Revolution. The Ten Commandments (i.e. — "Thou shalt not steal," "Thou shalt not kill,") provide a good example of this kind of thinking.

Standards of behavior are taught to children by their parents and other family members, by religious institutions, and by the schools they attend. As children learn and adopt such standards for themselves, they develop what Americans (and other Westerners) refer to as "conscience". This means knowing what is "right" to do and feeling that they should do it, even if no one is around to see. If they violate one of these divine laws or societal rules, Americans are taught that they should feel bad or guilty. Guilt is the feeling that one has done something wrong, that one has gone against a rule or standard. It is a feeling that one is not a good or worthwhile person because one hasn't lived up to one's own or to society's standards.

The desire not to feel guilty is a social means of control that keeps many Westerners doing the "right thing." The result is a society of formal and informal guidelines and laws in which people have accepted a large number of rules about what is right and what is wrong. These apply both to people they know and to people they don't know. Ideally, these rules are put into practice whether witnessed by anyone or not. (American crime and other social problems occur, in part, because people don't feel guilty for their actions. They don't see what they are doing as wrong. In these instances, the social control mechanism has broken down.)

The American ideal: It is more important to be right than to be liked

Americans customarily measure their behavior against what they think is the right thing to do. As long as they keep true to what they believe they should do, they do not feel guilty, regardless of the disapproval of others. In fact, to go against others' opinion, even those close to you such as family and friends when their thinking is contrary to what you believe is right, often is taken as the mark of a hero in American culture. America, you will remember, was settled by people who rejected the religious and political beliefs of Europe. They risked all for what they believed was right.

Americans, of course, are susceptible to the influence of others, particularly those close to them. Yet, to make decisions for yourself, by yourself, following your principles, is an American ideal. As an ideal, it is not always practiced, but it is the cultural value that enables Americans to go against the group, when they believe the group is wrong. This is very different from Asian cultural values which emphasize group harmony and responsiveness to group demands.

It is 1:00 a.m. and you are returning home from a party. As you proceed down the street, the traffic light ahead of you changes from green to red. There are no other cars on the road and no police in sight. What do you do?

**Americans
follow the
rules**

For Americans, the answer is simple. Almost all would stop. They believe that if everyone follows the rules or laws all will benefit. For example, if everyone consistently stops at the red traffic light, then all motorists and pedestrians will be safe and traffic will proceed in an orderly, predictable fashion. If drivers in the U.S. go through traffic lights, exceed the speed limit, or make turns from the wrong lane, they are likely to be stopped by the police (and get some rude gestures from fellow drivers). In Bangkok (or Manila, or Ho Chi Minh City), you may find a different situation. Many drivers will check to see if there are any vehicles coming or any police in sight. If not, they are likely to continue through the red light. This, they believe, facilitates the flow of traffic. They reason, "Why stop when it doesn't make any sense to do so?"

**Rules are
enforced
through
formal and
informal
means**

America is a land of rules and regulations. Americans proudly refer to their country as a society of laws. It is not surprising Americans have more lawyers per capita than any other nation in the world. In American society, there are a lot of "shoulds" and "musts", rules and regulations. Spoken and unspoken expectations about how you are supposed to behave are everywhere (i.e. "No smoking", "Don't litter", "Buckle your seat belt", "Stand in line", "Wait your turn"). They are enforced formally through police and other authorities and informally through expressions of disapproval. Break a commonly accepted social rule in the U.S. and you will get disapproving stares and a reminder to follow the rules (i.e. "I was in line ahead of you", "This is the non-smoking section. Please don't smoke"). Americans are taught to follow the rules and to apply them equally to all people, whether they are dealing with family, friends, or perfect strangers.

**When
Americans
break the
rules**

Having rules and following them make sense to Americans. It provides order and a sense of predictability. Americans, however, are not mindlessly devoted to rules and regulations. American individualism, discussed previously, helps to balance any tendency to blindly follow rules. That same individualism encourages them to question authority and examine the value and purpose of rules. If an American thinks that a rule or law is foolish or unjust, he will try to change, resist or ignore it. American history is full of examples, from the War of Independence to the Civil Rights Movement, of times when citizens have changed laws (rules) they felt were wrong.

An American commuting to work in Jakarta experiences the daily frustration of driving in a crowded Asian city. From his perspective, people honk their horns too much, cut him off too often, and drive too close to his car. He tries to turn into a busy intersection, but no one allows him the opportunity to edge in. As another car is about to cut him off, he notices that the driver is his Indonesian neighbor. He makes eye contact with his neighbor. Instead of cutting him off, his neighbor, with a gallant wave of his hand, slows his car to allow the American to enter the stream of traffic. The American has moved from the "out" group (the public, the unknown, the stranger) to the "in" group. The Indonesian wouldn't think of being impolite or inconsiderate to someone he knows.

"In" group vs. "Out" group behavior

Many Asian cultures look at social rules quite differently from American culture. In most group-based cultures, everyone fits into one of three categories: 1) people who are within your important groups (family, friends, schoolmates, etc.); 2) people with whom you have contact on a regular basis and who are in your social network (work colleagues, neighbors, etc); and 3) everyone else. In most Asian cultures, there are very rigid codes of conduct about how to act towards people in the first two categories. These people are in the "in" group in a shame-based culture. They are people you know, people who know you, and people with whom you must maintain harmonious relationships. Inappropriate, impolite, or uncaring behavior towards these people brings shame or loss of face to you and your group.

The third category includes people who are unknown, people who are strangers. They are often treated as nonpersons, almost as if they do not exist. They do not fit into any meaningful groups or social networks. Therefore, the very rigid codes of conduct and social etiquette that apply to people in the first two categories do not apply to them.

Americans are often puzzled by Asians' public behavior

For Americans visiting or living in Asia, this distinction between "in" and "out" group behavior is, perhaps, one of the most difficult things for them to understand about Asian cultures. They interact with Asians socially as well as at work and find them to be among the kindest, most considerate, and polite people they have ever met. Then, they meet other Asians in a public situation (on a bus, driving in traffic, in the market) and see them as rude, impolite, and inconsiderate. They wonder how people from the same culture can behave so differently. Generally, Americans do not realize that there are different rules for those you know, the "in" group, and those you don't know, the "out" group. Coming from a guilt-based society, Americans believe that there shouldn't be any distinction in how you treat those you know and those you don't know. Public behavior should be guided by a set of rules which apply to all. Ideally, in these situations, you should treat everyone equally.

Business Applications

Rules at Work

Mrs. Huang has worked for the company for eight years in Taipei. She comes to her supervisor one day and asks for one month's leave. Her son is preparing for the university examinations and she wants to be home to be sure he eats well, is not disturbed, and focuses on his studies.

If her supervisor is Chinese, he is likely to say: "Take the time off." He thinks, "Mrs. Huang has been with our company for a long time. She is a good worker and has a long future with us. This time is important to her. It would be heartless not to give her a few extra weeks."

If her supervisor is American, he is likely to say: "Mrs. Huang, you have already taken all your leave for this year. I know this is important to you and I'm very sorry, but I can't give you any extra leave." He thinks, "If I make an exception for Mrs. Huang, then tomorrow I will have Mr. Wang asking for extra leave to visit his mother, and the next day Ms. Tsai will come with some other issue. The situation will get out of control. I can't let that happen."

The Asian leader is benevolent and humane

The ideal Asian leader or boss is one who leads by example and maintains the highest standards of moral excellence. This concept of moral excellence may be translated as character, kindness, benevolence, or humaneness. Ideally, the leader is courteous, sympathetic, and caring in words and actions to all subordinates at all times.

When making a decision like the one above where an employee asks for extra leave, the Asian leader, as a rule, measures it against one of three possible standards: 1) what is the humane, kind, or caring choice; 2) what is the rational, customary, or traditional way to handle the situation; or 3) what does the rule or law say. Traditionally, in most Asian cultures, the best way to make a decision is on the basis of benevolence or caring; the worst way is to rely on laws, rules, or regulations.

Formalized, detailed rules, in traditional Asian thinking, are harmful to human relationships.

The American follows the rules

For Americans, rules, laws, or regulations are the best way to make decisions. In American business, it is important to comply with policies and standard operating procedures. Americans believe such policies and procedures ensure fairness to everyone. They can be applied consistently and uniformly. They are predictable. Asian benevolence or humaneness is seen by many American managers as the least desirable standard to use in making decisions. To Americans, viewed through their cultural glasses (with lenses that emphasize fairness and equality), this often looks like favoritism, unfairness, or corruption. Americans ask, "How can you treat one person differently from another?" "How can you make a decision without consistent guidelines that apply equally to all?"

Standards for Making a Decision
(in order of priority)

	Asians		*Americans*
1.	Benevolence/ humaneness/ kindness	1.	Rules/laws
2.	Customs/ traditions/ rational thinking	2.	Customs/ traditions/ rational thinking
3.	Rules/laws	3.	Benevolence/ humaneness/ kindness

Americans can be quite insistent on following the rules, even at times when the rules may not make much sense. They have been taught that if everyone follows the rules, all will benefit. If people break or "bend" the rules, chaos will result. Control and predictability will be lost. They can become very uncomfortable or frustrated when the rules are not heeded, particularly in the areas of safety and quality control. They are reluctant to make exceptions to rules, fearing that doing so will set precedents forcing them to allow the same exceptions for anyone else who asks. Americans say, "Rules are meant to be followed."

What This Means For You:

Pay special attention to rules, policies, and safety regulations in an American organization. Breaking rules, even ones that don't seem to make sense, can get you dismissed from an American company.

Contracts

The buying office for a large American department store places a U.S.\$500,000 order with a factory in Thailand to have merchandise on the docks for shipment to the U.S. in one month. The standard contract requires the factory owner to air freight the shipment to the U.S. if his dockside delivery is late. Two weeks before the due date, the factory owner informs his American colleague that there has been a disastrous fire at the factory. He quickly states, however, that he is aware of how important this shipment is. He has rented additional equipment, borrowed the upper floor of his brother's factory, and hired extra staff to work overtime. He implies, but does not state, that he will not be able to meet the contract deadline. He expects that his American buyer will see he is doing all he possibly can to meet his obligations, but that this tragedy was something out of his control. He assumes he will not be charged for the air freight. The American, while very sympathetic to his supplier's difficulties, feels his hands are tied. The contract was signed, trucks are scheduled to be at the dock in Los Angeles for the shipment on the assigned arrival date for distribution throughout the U.S.A., and the home office would never approve renegotiating the contract at this stage.

*The
importance
of the
written word*

For Americans, the written word carries more meaning than anything spoken or implied. When compared to what is said, letters, agendas, minutes, and memos carry a greater sense of importance, formality, power, and urgency. In general, Americans use this form of communication more frequently and with greater ease than their Asian counterparts. Written communication meets their needs for documented and clear records of what happened, what is happening, or what will happen. It allows all involved to start from the same place, with the same shared information. It brings control, order and predictability to the business world.

*Contracts
have
different
meanings
for Asians
and
Americans*

One area of considerable cross-cultural misunderstanding between East and West revolves around the meaning, use, and handling of business contracts. To a traditional Asian manager, a handshake or verbal agreement with someone you know, who is duty-bound to honor his commitment, is more binding than some words on paper. A written contract is often viewed as a statement of intention, what one hopes to do, if at all possible. It serves as the intermediate point between initial negotiations and final delivery of goods or services. Because conditions can always change, and any one individual cannot control or predict the future, the contract can only be a goal, not a firm commitment of what will definitely happen. As a display of faith in the relationship, contracts may be renegotiated when something goes badly for one of the contractors. Because of these factors, written business contracts in Asia traditionally have been less important than verbal agreements and, when written, have been limited in details.

*For
Americans,
contracts
are end
points*

To an American manager, a contract is typically seen as the end point of a process. Each contract is a separate and distinct agreement that requires the contractors to perform specific tasks over a set period of time. The contractual relationship is seen as a time-bound arrangement. It carries with it no obligations to develop personal relationships or to continue doing business beyond the contractual period. Because of the legalistic orientation of American society, it is assumed that a contract will be fulfilled exactly as it has been written. If it is not, the courts will enforce the appropriate penalties. This is why Americans want to "close the deal", sign the contract, before they depart from their Asian business trip.

While contracts can be, and are, renegotiated, that is not the normal way of doing business for Americans. They believe that, if you make a "bad" contract (not in your favor), you must live with the consequences. They often are confused and frustrated when Asians in business want to bring up contractual adjustments after an agreement has been signed. From their point of view, discussion time is over and the job now is to carry out the terms of the contract. For the traditional Asian businessman, the contract is just one, isolated agreement in a long-term relationship, a relationship that should be characterized by understanding, support, and mutual dependency.

Generally, the American businessperson wants to put all possible contingencies (things that can go wrong) in a contract. American contracts are full of fine print detailing every possible point of future disagreement. Americans want to be "covered" for all possible events that may arise. It's no wonder that American business contracts can be lengthy, full of detail, and practically unreadable, even to a native English speaker.

Ethics

A poor boy is caught stealing food from the market. He is brought before the judge. Before sentencing, the judge asks him why he stole. The boy answers by saying his parents are poor and hungry. He stole the food for them. Many traditional Asians would agree that the boy was fulfilling his duty to his parents. To do otherwise in the situation would be unethical. Many traditional Americans would sympathize with the boy's situation. Nonetheless, many would affirm that, "Stealing is never right, no matter what," and see the boy's behavior as unethical (as well as illegal).

*Ethics define
appropriate
behavior*

Ethics in business are a set of guidelines or moral principles that assist members of an organization to determine the right course of action. They are codes of conduct defining right and wrong. They provide instructions for how to respond in different situations.

In many Asian societies, the traditional view regarding law and ethics has been that such crimes as murder, disobeying the Sultan, King or Emperor, or aiding the enemy, were very serious and brought clear and swift penalties. Many other matters, not seen as a direct threat to society, were best left to the subjective handling of the people and officials involved. Abstract principles of right and wrong were less important than day-to-day survival and maintenance of the group. Ethics were situational and depended upon the specific circumstances and the nature of the relationship of those involved. Ethics, traditionally, were more related to benevolence and humaneness than to rules and laws.

To the rule-following American, there are clear, universal guidelines that apply equally to all, regardless of relationships. There is right and wrong. You are either honest or dishonest, truthful or deceptive. It is very important for the American in business to act and to be seen to act in a way that is ethical. Most American business schools provide some sort of training in this area. What is, then, ethical and unethical from the American perspective?

Your company's product lies on the dock. To avoid spoilage and to get it to market, you need to transport it quickly. The customs official suggests that a "gift" to him and his staff would facilitate getting the necessary approvals. What do you do?

One definition of ethical behavior in business involves not doing anything unlawful or improper that will harm the organization. It revolves around the American values of fairness, equality, and following the rules. Americans are likely to view actions which favor one individual or group at the expense of other individuals, groups, or society as a whole, as wrong or unethical. They are likely to use negative words like "bribery" or "corruption" when faced with a decision to engage in or allow behavior which favors the "in" group and puts the "out" group at a disadvantage. By that we mean any action — from not paying taxes to not following legal environmental standards — which benefit an individual, group or company, but is at the expense of other individuals, groups, or the society at large. Americans would say, "It's not fair or right."

Gifts or bribes?

For example, many American companies have clear corporate policies on giving and receiving gifts. It is believed that business decisions should be made only on the basis of what is best for the company and should not break the law of the U.S. or the host country. Accepting a gift from a contractor, for example, creates a debt to the giver which could result in favoritism when a contract decision is to be made. The result, American managers believe, is that the company loses because the decision could be made on the basis of personal obligations and relationships and not on the merit of the offering or the best price. If allowed to continue and grow unchecked, this type of behavior, most Americans believe, can only lead to disaster for the company. For this reason, many large American companies require employees to read and sign documents acknowledging that they are aware of the company's policy and severe penalties (often dismissal) for giving or receiving gifts from suppliers, government officials, or contractors. The same situation as the one presented above, through Asian cultural glasses, may simply be seen as the obligation to take care of someone who takes care of you.

> ### *What This Means For You:*
>
> *Pay careful attention to the codes of conduct and ethical standards in your organization. Expect the rule-following American supervisor to be both upset with, and intolerant of, behavior which goes against the ethical standards of your company.*

Some behaviors that generally would be seen by Americans as unethical at work include:

- Using company assets or relationships for personal gain.
- Failing to respect the intellectual property rights either of your company or of other companies/individuals.
- Failing to maintain the confidentiality of corporate, client, and employee information.
- Making false claims for products or services (truth in advertising).
- Having a financial interest in the business of a competitor or supplier, or receiving payment (in cash or in gifts) for assistance given (conflict of interest).
- Lying or providing false or misleading information to people to whom you report (i.e. superiors, stockholders, tax authorities).
- Failure to set or enforce adequate standards for product or workplace safety.
- Failure to report the illegal activities of other workers of which you are aware.

Negotiation

For a number of months, a large American advertising company was discussing the possibility of buying a small Japanese company so as to have a foothold in the Japanese market. The American CEO saw the merger as a positive one for both sides and thought the time was right to send over a negotiating team comprised of the company lawyer and his Vice-President for International Marketing to "close the deal".

The American negotiating team arrived in Tokyo on Sunday. They hoped they could come to terms by Wednesday or Friday at the latest. They wanted to get right down to detailed negotiations and didn't understand the daily invitations to lunch and dinner extended by their Japanese negotiating partners. They assumed dinner and drinks, once the negotiations had been successfully concluded, would be sufficient. By Thursday, they were still far apart on a final agreement. The Americans, frustrated with what they saw as lack of movement, told the Japanese negotiating team that they had to see some progress on major issues which they could take back with them when they left on Friday.

Even though both the Japanese and the Americans were genuinely interested in the merger, the talks failed to bring the two sides closer together. Both the Japanese and the Americans left the negotiations thinking the other side had been most unreasonable.

Different cultures have different negotiating styles

Much has been written about different national styles of negotiation. There are literally hundreds of books currently in print in the U.S. offering tips on how to negotiate with the Japanese, the Chinese and other Asians. The American manager who deals with Asians has a considerable amount of interest in this topic. For many, this is the first (and sometimes the only) time when he or she will meet face-to-face with someone from a radically different culture. Similarly, this may be the only time an Asian executive deals directly with his or her American counterpart.

Asian styles of negotiating: Common themes

There is a considerable amount of difference in negotiating styles between and among various Asian cultures. There are, however, some important commonalities. The way people approach negotiation is a reflection of the way they approach business in general. For most Asians, the focus of the negotiation process tends to be on the long-term possibilities that can come out of the relationship, rather than the specific transaction that is being discussed. In Asia, the goal is that everyone should win. A relationship of trust must be established before you can do business. Therefore, negotiations often begin on the personal and general level and only proceed to specific issues once it has been established that significant mutual interest exists. Issues may be discussed in any order and decisions on all issues are generally not made until near the conclusion of negotiations.

Most agreements are made informally in meetings held before or in-between the formal negotiating sessions. Participants rarely are backed into a corner. There normally is a face-saving way out for everyone. As decisions in Asian business are made by the group or the top person rather than the individual who holds the functional responsibility, Asian negotiations take longer, and negotiating positions are only shifted after consultations between or after bargaining sessions.

The outcome of a successful negotiation is consensus on mutually shared issues. Specific details may or may not be resolved. It is assumed that if the the overall structure is in place, the details can be worked out over time.

Expect a range of negotiating styles from Americans

While Americans have become much more sophisticated and culturally-sensitive in negotiating with Asians over the last few decades, their traditional style of negotiation can potentially open the door to cross-cultural misunderstanding. While you may find yourself dealing with an American who is quite sophisticated in cross-cultural negotiations, you may also find yourself working with a more tradition-bound American.

Traditional American negotiating

Traditionally, American negotiating styles have been characterized by those very values that underpin American society and American business. They include:

1)   **"Win-Lose" Orientation:**
Despite the fact that current American management thinking encourages the use of a win-win perspective, negotiating for the typical American is often seen as a competitive, rather than cooperative, venture. The traditional cultural perspective emphasizes coming out ahead, beating your opponent. Looking for the best deal often results in a win-lose orientation in which American negotiators strive to get the best short-term gains, sometimes overlooking or ignoring the benefits of a long-term relationship.

2)   **"Get Results" Orientation:**
Americans want to focus on the issues and get the negotiation accomplished in a short period of time. They want discussion that gets to the point, to the heart of the issues, quickly. They can become impatient with long, drawn-out negotiations. They may try to push their Asian colleagues to make a decision faster than those colleagues are ready to move. ("This is our final offer.") They are reluctant to take "no" for an answer and equally reluctant for negotiations to end inconclusively or with no decision having been made. Their style may be perceived by the Asian negotiator as overly-direct and even aggressive, especially when the American negotiator is persistent (wants to close the deal now) and doesn't see or heed the Asian signals indicating that it is time to back off.

On the other hand, Asian negotiators may use American impatience to their advantage. Americans sometimes may give in on points in order to finish the negotiation process and move on to other business.

3)   **"Lay Your Cards on the Table" Orientation:**
The basic strategy for much of American negotiation revolves around the principle, "You

tell me what you want, I'll tell you what I want and we'll proceed from there." Americans expect a degree of clarity, directness, and openness of intention at the bargaining table. (This, of course, does not mean that American negotiators don't keep some information to themselves as bargaining chips for later rounds of negotiating.) They want straight answers. They want to know where they stand. They expect clear "yes" or "no" responses to their proposals. This can be frustrating and embarrassing for the Asian negotiator who either is not in the position to make the decision (at that time or without consultation with others) or who is uncomfortable verbalizing a clear and direct "no".

4)   **"One-at-a-Time" Orientation:**
Americans approach a complex negotiation by breaking down the issues that need to be addressed into a series of sub-issues or parts. They look to settle each part, one at a time, in a sequential or logical order. Emphasis is placed upon being able to justify each position with a persuasive set of background information and statistics.

5)   **"Equality/Informality" Orientation:**
The American value of equality and informality in human relations results in minimizing status differences around the conference table. The American negotiator may say, "Let's not stand on ceremony (the form and ritual). Let's just get on with it." This may make it confusing to the Asian negotiator as to who is in charge and where the process of negotiation is heading.

6)   **"Individualistic Decision-Making" Orientation:**
American negotiators often take an individualistic approach, preferring to go it alone

or to include very few others on their team. They expect that decisions will be reached at the negotiating table. They usually have the authority to make final commitments or agreements, unlike their Asian counterparts who often must check with the home office, their superiors, or the entire group for consensus. American negotiators may be frustrated with the inability to come to a decision at the time of negotiation. Asian negotiators may be frustrated with the confrontational or aggressive style used by Americans in trying to push for a decision.

7)   **"Legalistic" Orientation:**
American negotiators want to conclude the deal with a very precise written contract or agreement. Expect that contracts will be detailed and lengthy. The contract is the end point of the negotiation process. It is assumed it will be followed exactly as written by both parties.

8)   **Other Negotiation Strategies:**
While there is a range of strategies Americans regularly employ, there are some common themes that seem to come up again and again. Americans tend to place more emphasis on narrowing areas of difference rather than on finding areas of agreement, of identifying and focussing on problem areas rather than areas of commonality. They believe that progress is made by getting down to the details of the issues involved. A successful negotiation results in a deal acceptable to both parties in which specific and concrete terms are set out in detail. Generally, they don't expect to spend as much time discussing the overall framework or establishing the relationship between the parties as is commonly the case in Asia.

When negotiating price, Americans often will begin the negotiation process at a price not very far from what they want and expect to get. In contrast, their Asian counterparts often will start with a price well beyond what they are willing to accept. As a result, Americans often leave themselves much less bargaining room than the typical Asian negotiator and are often dismayed by the Asian negotiator's seemingly "unreasonable" initial bargaining position.

Americans tend to make concessions only reluctantly at first, saving their major concessions until the later parts of the negotiation session. When negotiations are not progressing as fast or smoothly as they expect, Americans may use threats or warnings to generate some movement in the negotiation process. There may come a time in the negotiation where they will tell their negotiating partners to "take it or leave it", meaning not to expect any further concessions.

What This Means For You:

In both the areas of contracts and negotiations, you may be able to be very helpful to your American colleagues by serving as a cross-cultural guide, helping them to understand the thinking and behavior of those from your culture in these important business transactions.

10
Communicating with Americans

Mr. Sanchez, an American CEO in Korea, passes one of his managers, Mr. Kim, in the hall as he is on his way to a meeting. He says, "Hey Kim, how about that report you're working on for marketing. Doesn't the Sales Department want it soon?" Mr. Kim is not sure what his boss means. Is he <u>informing</u> him? ("A report is needed by Sales.") Is he <u>directing</u> him? ("You should get the report to them now.") Is he <u>questioning</u> him? ("Does Sales want the report soon?") Or, is he making a <u>suggestion</u>? ("I suggest we think about getting the report out in the near future.")

Communication makes things happen

Studies have shown that 75 percent of what good managers do each day is communicate (Harris & Moran, 1991). This involves talking to other staff, writing reports, memos and proposals, and, most importantly, listening to the ideas, suggestions, and reactions of colleagues. Communication is one of the most valuable and important tools we have for getting things done. It is also the most common way we cause each other frustration.

Communication is not easy, especially across cultures

Communicating effectively with someone of your own culture is not always easy. When people are upset, rushed, or uncomfortable in a situation, they may not say what they really intended to say. Or, the person listening may give a very different meaning to what is said than what the speaker meant. There are many times when people who share common values, backgrounds, and experiences as us fail to get the message we send. When different cultural values and assumptions, different styles of communication, as well as language barriers are added, communication across cultures can become very complicated.

When Mr. Sanchez from New York wants to communicate with his Asian colleague, Mr. Kim from Seoul, he first has to translate ① what he wants to say, into a message format ② — words, gestures, a written note, etc. The message then must be received ③ by Mr. Kim who has to figure out what the message means.

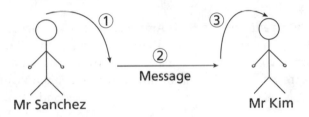

This process sounds pretty simple. In reality, it is quite complicated and full of possibilities for misunderstanding. What makes it difficult are the different rules and glasses utilized by Mr. Sanchez and Mr. Kim. More accurately, the diagram should look like this:

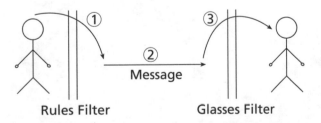

Mr. Sanchez comes to the situation with certain rules on how to express his thoughts and feelings. Whether it is a personal compliment, a business proposal, feedback, or a question, his culture has taught him the "appropriate" or right way to put these ideas or emotions into a message. Mr. Kim's culture has also taught him rules or the "right" way to give praise, suggest ideas, give feedback, or pose a question. The two translations for the very same thought or feeling may be very different messages. At the other end, the receiver of the message has to translate what he sees, hears, or reads. He has to make sense of the message. He can only do this by processing what he sees or hears through his own cultural glasses or filters. The result, of course, is a high potential for miscommunication or cross-cultural missing when trying to communicate with someone of a different culture. The solution? Become more aware of your own culture's communication rules as well as those of the people with whom you work.

Pay attention to communication patterns

Both American and Asian managers need to work on this critical area. Americans, most of whom have never had to learn a second language, find themselves at a disadvantage when communicating with someone who speaks English as a second (or third or fourth) language. The Asian working in an American multinational company knows there are different styles and patterns of communication. Some American colleagues may still be learning this important lesson. To be effective, both sides need to be aware of cultural differences in communication and to style-switch, when necessary.

Cultures in Contrast: Asian vs. American Styles of Communicating

Mr. Phillips:	"How long will you need to finish the project report you are working on?"
(Phillips thinks:	I need to get this information for planning purposes.)
(Wang thinks:	Why is he asking me this?)
Mr. Wang:	"I do not know. When do you want it?"
(Phillips thinks:	Why doesn't he know? He's in the best position to know.)
(Wang thinks:	He's the boss. He should tell me when he wants it.)
Mr. Phillips:	"I need it as soon as possible. Can you get it to me in two weeks?"
(Phillips thinks:	I need to press him on this project or else it will never get done.)
(Wang thinks:	I am working as hard as I can. I'm not sure when it will be done. It will depend on what other projects and demands come my way.)
Mr. Wang:	"Yes. I will finish it in two weeks."
(Phillips thinks:	Great! We finally have a firm deadline. I don't have to worry about this anymore.)
(Wang thinks:	He wanted a date so I agreed. I don't want him to get upset. I will try my best to meet it.)

In fact, the project report objectively required three weeks of work to be completed. Mr. Wang worked overtime to get the job done, but by the end of the second week he was still two days short of completing the report.

| Mr. Phillips: | "Where is the project report? You agreed it would be ready today." |

(Phillips thinks: *I must make sure he complies with his commitment. I can't trust Wang to do what he says he will do.*)

(Wang thinks: *Can't he see I've almost killed myself trying to meet his timeline, which was unrealistic in the first place? This is an impossible man to work for!*)

Asian communication style

For Asians like Mr. Wang, communication is meant to facilitate good interpersonal relationships. It is designed to promote and maintain harmony. Because of this, the "how" of communication is as important as the "what" of communication. The way something is said is as important as what is said.

As we have seen previously, in Asian societies great effort usually is made to minimize open disagreement. Indirectness helps promote harmony by minimizing the chances of conflict. When communicating bad news or dealing with a problem, Asians will often use a neutral or respected third party to reduce loss of face. No matter what is talked about, Asians emphasize politeness, courtesy, and respect . Threatening words or tones are rarely used. Asians realize that good communication takes time. They make taking that time a priority in their lives.

In many Asian languages, a word or phrase makes sense only when it is viewed in the light of what comes before it and what follows after it. While Asians pay careful attention to the words, they also learn to pay attention to the context of a word — the information that surrounds the specific word (the voice tone, gestures, even the words which aren't said) — for its meaning to come to life. Words can be vague, have multiple meanings, or different interpretations. It is from the context that the meaning comes.

American communication style

For Americans like Mr. Phillips, communication is a tool to get something done. The words carry most of the message and the meaning. Americans focus attention on what is said or written. They generally are less concerned and pay less attention to the information that surrounds the words — the voice tone, the body language of the speaker, what was said before, and what follows after — than do their Asian colleagues.

While words are more important than non-verbal means of communication for the average American, written words are more important than those that are merely spoken. In American business, contracts, standard operating procedures, performance appraisals, cost estimates, and much more are all written down. If something is important, Americans will say, "Put it in writing."

Communication for Americans should be as clear and as precise as possible. Americans want to reduce the chances of misunderstanding, of people receiving different meanings from the same message. In business, communication based on facts and logic is valued. Communication that is concise and brief, that says what you intend to say and doesn't waste another's time, is seen as relevant and useful. Americans, therefore, place great emphasis on memos and reports to ensure that information gets communicated in a concise, clear manner and that everyone involved gets the same message.

Americans talk a lot

There are other aspects of the typical American style of communicating that Asians sometimes find strange, confusing, or frustrating. Americans may talk a lot. They have been trained to be verbal from an early age. Their schooling has reinforced the importance of speaking up and speaking out. They are comfortable with words and engaging others in discussion. They fill silences with questions or their own comments when Asians hesitate or take time to think before speaking. They often dominate discussions and are accused of speaking more than listening. Asians sometimes are overwhelmed by the flood of words they receive from Americans. Because America is such a verbal culture where words are so important, Americans believe that participation and involvement means speaking. If someone does not talk, then he or she is not seen as participating.

> **What This Means For You:**
>
> *To be seen as involved and contributing, you need to voice your ideas and questions. You need to make your voice heard.*

The American style of informal conversation is like a ping-pong match. It moves back and forth between participants, with each person taking turns to talk. No one person should dominate the conversation. All present should have an equal chance to speak. They may interrupt another speaker from time to time to move the conversation along or to give their opinion. This may be seen as quite impolite from the perspective of many Asians.

Americans ask a lot of questions

Americans tend to ask a lot of questions. They want to get all the information they possibly can on a subject of interest or concern. Having as much relevant information as possible will help them make the best choice or decision. Also, Americans frequently ask a lot of questions just to keep a conversation moving. Sometimes, this can feel like an interrogation to an Asian, with one question following the other.

When Americans ask a question, they expect an answer right away. If they don't get a response, they may assume that the person is angry, bored or just has nothing to say. In that case, they fill the silence with another question or make a statement of their own.

> **What This Means For You:**
>
> *If you are asked a question by an American and need some time to think of your answer, you need to give some indication you are forming your response. Americans in this situation will typically say such things as:*
>
> > *"Let me see . . ." "Hold on . . ."*
> > *"Um . . ." "Let me think about this."*
> > *"Just give me a minute . . ."*
> > *"Uh, how can I say this . . ."*
>
> *These are signals to the American to give you time to think.*

Argument and debate

Argument and debate, taking positions in opposition for the sake of discussion, are not unusual in American business meetings. American executives sometimes will play the "devil's advocate". This means that they will disagree with a proposal or idea, presenting counter-arguments and questions, just to be sure that the issue has been explored fully before a decision is made. Americans believe they can disagree about ideas and still like each other and work effectively together. As a result, heated disagreement, while not intentional, does not feel as bad to them as it might to Asian managers.

Business Applications

Communicating Emotions

Three months ago, Khun Preecha, a Thai manager, feared that his colleague, Mr. Kramer, would jeopardize their project because he displayed his anger when speaking to their American superiors about making some improvements and correcting some problems. True, Mr. Kramer did not completely lose his temper, but still, it was easy to see that he was not as calm and respectful as he should have been. Now Khun Preecha is confused to find that, rather than suffering by letting his emotions become obvious, Mr. Kramer has been given a bonus for his suggestions and seems to be held in higher regard.

Culture influences emotions

Everyone experiences emotions. What triggers these emotions and the way emotions are expressed differ across cultures. Also, there are personality as well as cultural differences which influence how comfortable people are in showing others how they feel.

Asians admire people who can restrain emotions and keep interpersonal relations smooth because emotions can be dangerous if they get out of control. The leader who displays self-control in words, gestures, and tone is admired in Asian cultures. Most Thais, like many other Asians, will talk approvingly of the person who is *cai yen* (cool heart) and will look down on the person who is *cai rawn* (hot heart) — quick to express anger or impatience. There are many proverbs throughout Asia like the Thai one, "Keep muddy waters inside while you keep clear waters outside," (Fieg, 1989). Such sayings encourage people to keep communication smooth and free from unpleasant emotions.

Americans show emotions in public

American communication can be filled with emotion. While not as fiery as Arabs or Latin Americans, Americans can be quite emotional in their style of communicating when compared with most Asians. For the most part, Americans in business do not approve of showing too much emotion. They are more comfortable with logic and with keeping communication "businesslike", that is, unemotional. However, you will see Americans at work display impatience, annoyance, frustration, even anger through their voice tone, their gestures, and their words. With the possible exception of Koreans, most Asians are taught not to show emotions, particularly negative emotions, in public. Americans, on the other hand, learn that it is acceptable to display emotions, within limits.

Of course there is a wide range among Americans when it comes to expressing emotions. Some differences are based on age. Others reflect differences between the sexes. Still others result from differences in cultural background. Nevertheless, Americans generally believe that a frank and open discussion of feelings is better than keeping one's feelings hidden inside. They believe it "clears the air" and allows people to get on with the tasks at hand, without the negative effects of strong, hidden emotions. They encourage people to express their feelings with phrases such as, "Get if off your chest", "Talk it out", "Don't hold it in". Generally, they believe that expressing emotions helps people to get rid of them. They talk about being able to "forgive and forget", after an argument or disagreement. Americans often talk about feeling "good" after letting negative emotions out. For them, emotions are like the steam trapped in a covered teapot, ready to cause an explosion. If the top is taken off the teapot, some of the steam escapes and an explosion is prevented. While Americans may see "letting off steam" as a way of making communication more effective, Asians may see the very same behavior as a lack of self-control and a clear block to effective communication.

What This Means For You:

It is not uncommon for American managers to ask, "What's wrong?" if they see by your

> *expression or voice tone that something is disturbing you. They expect you will talk about it with them, rather than keeping it inside. If you say that everything is "fine", the American manager will assume either that there is no problem or that the problem is not one which you want to discuss.*
>
> *Generally, Americans are not very good at reading Asians' non-verbal expressions. Therefore, if you are upset but do not directly express it, they may not notice that anything is the matter.*

Truth vs. Courtesy

Mr. Raymont's Chinese work colleagues complimented him upon news of his promotion and suggested he should treat them all to a dinner. Mr. Raymont smiled, but said nothing. He didn't know how to respond to his colleagues' suggestion. That afternoon, he had the opportunity to talk with Mr. Tsai who had advised him a number of times on Chinese culture. Mr. Raymont told Mr. Tsai about the conversation and asked how he should respond. Mr. Tsai smiled and explained that it was a Chinese custom to suggest a dinner to celebrate good fortune and that the best way to respond would be to say something like, "Yes, of course I will treat you all to dinner," whether you really intend to or not. Mr. Raymont thought for a moment and said, "I can't do that." "Why not?" asked a puzzled Mr. Tsai. "That wouldn't be honest," answered Mr. Raymont. Mr. Tsai smiled with understanding and replied, "This doesn't have anything to do with honesty. It's about politeness."

A priority for Asians ... saving face

Most Asians have been taught that paying attention to another's feelings or sensitivities during a conversation is more important than communicating an objective truth. In the long run, saving face and keeping communication smooth usually is a higher priority than getting any one task or job accomplished. In some instances, an employee would rather suffer in silence than confront his boss with an issue. An employee may prefer not to acknowledge to his boss that he doesn't understand instructions rather than to admit this and to suffer a loss of face. As a result, Asians may often be more reluctant than their American counterparts to convey bad or disappointing news. Saying they don't understand, disagreeing, or sharing an unpleasant truth can be difficult. Disharmony in communication is to be avoided, if at all possible.

When Americans prefer politeness over truth

Americans, on the other hand, have been taught that communication should be truthful. In dealing with issues of importance, Americans usually believe that "truth" is more important than feelings. If an issue is one of little significance or is a matter of courtesy, Americans, like their Asian counterparts, are likely to engage in "white lies" to save the face and not hurt the feelings of those involved. For example, a friend may ask, "What do you think of my new haircut?" Wanting to be polite, the American will answer (just like most Asians), "It looks great," even if it doesn't.

When Americans prefer truth over politeness

The difference between Asians and Americans becomes more apparent on issues considered to be of greater importance. In the area of work, getting the job done, as we have seen, is considered by the average American to have a higher priority than preserving the face of colleagues or subordinates. While Indonesian, Malaysian, or Filipino employees may be reluctant to share news with the boss which they know will be disappointing, Americans would see it as their responsibility to get that information to the boss as soon as possible, so that new plans could be made and any losses minimized.

Americans will give negative feedback, share unpleasant news, or disagree far more easily and far more often than their Asian counterparts. They see being honest and truthful as the way to overcome obstacles and to get a job done. They are more comfortable at doing that, having been trained from an early age to do so. They don't believe the impact on face and harmony to be nearly as serious as their Asian colleagues.

> **What This Means For You:**
>
> *Americans can be painfully honest. There isn't much you can do about this, except to remember that, generally, their intention in behaving in this way is to improve the situation, not to hurt you.*

Being Direct

Mr. Klein, the manager of an American company in Indonesia notices that Ms. Hadiwijono, who is normally cheerful, seems quiet and withdrawn. He asks her if there is anything wrong and she tells him that nothing is the matter. A few days later, however, Mr. Sumitro approaches Mr. Klein on Ms. Hadiwijono's behalf. He mentions how well he thinks Ms. Hadiwijono is doing and what an asset she is to the company. He advises Mr. Klein that she is unhappy because she feels she did not get a deserved raise. Mr. Klein appreciates understanding the situation, but is puzzled by Ms. Hadiwijono's reluctance to speak to him directly about the matter.

Asians are indirect

Asians have a tendency to be indirect, especially when addressing a problem area. Often, they will talk about a different issue and then carefully guide the discussion to touch upon the difficult issue, never addressing it clearly or directly. Asians who are listening to this conversation are able to "read between the lines." They can pick up the subtle clues from this indirect message and clearly understand what is being communicated. Americans, listening to this same conversation, paying attention primarily to the words that are spoken, can easily fail to "hear" the message that is really being communicated.

Americans may feel frustrated when communicating with an Asian because they are unsure of where they stand:

What is the Asian really trying to communicate? Has the Asian received their message? What's going to happen next? Many Americans are not very good at reading between the lines. They often do not hear the issue or problem. Alternatively, Asians may get frustrated in communicating with Americans because they can't understand why their "clear" communication is not being received by the Americans, why the Americans are so insensitive to what is so obvious to them and their other Asian colleagues.

> **What This Means For You:**
>
> *Americans may not "hear" the message behind a polite, indirect communication. It helps if you start out by clearly defining what you want to discuss. You might begin with something like, "I'd like to talk to you about . . ." or "There's an issue we need to discuss." (Name the issue.)*

**Americans
are direct**

Americans usually are very direct in their communication. They want you to "get to the point". They believe people should state openly and directly what they think and what they want from other people. They are impatient with people who "beat around the bush", or "go around in circles" (don't say clearly and concisely what they mean).

> **What This Means For You:**
>
> *When reporting the results of a project, a meeting, sales, or other similar business activities to American supervisors or colleagues, keep your presentation short and to the point. Let the Americans know right away the most important outcomes. If they want more details, they will ask for them.*

Here's another example of how American directness and Asian politeness may cause problems. While Americans may say, "You must . . . " or "You are required to . . . ", Asians are more likely to say, "May I suggest . . . " or "We would appreciate. . .", to show respect and politeness. Asians may be offended by the American's directness or bluntness which may come across as a rude order; Americans may misinterpret Asians' gentle requests as not being really urgent or important and, therefore, not requiring immediate action. If the Americans later learn that the request was, in fact, a requirement, they may become angry or frustrated. They might reason, "If this was a requirement, why didn't you just say so?" Not being clear and direct is often seen by Americans as somewhat dishonest . Even if they don't get angry, they are likely to be upset because they see indirectness or vagueness as terribly inefficient when they are trying to get something done.

(While most American managers are normally direct, there are times when this is not the case. This occurs most often when the issue is personal, embarrassing or they are uncertain about how the other person may react.)

Communicating Agreement and Disagreement: Saying "Yes" and Saying "No"

A Filipino manager is talking to a colleague about his American boss: "My boss asked me to work overtime this weekend to finish the budget proposal before our meetings next week. I really didn't want to because my niece is getting married this weekend. I mentioned this to the boss a few weeks ago. When he asked me this morning to work this weekend, I said "Yes," even though I really didn't want to do it. Why couldn't he see how I felt or remember this important date for my family?

If the American boss could have heard this discussion, he probably would have responded with something like, "Why didn't you tell me you couldn't work this weekend? When you said 'yes' to my request,

*I assumed you were able to get the work done and attend the wedding.
How am I to know what you can and can't do if you don't tell me?"*

Communicating agreement or disagreement is an area
filled with great potential for cross-cultural
misunderstanding. Asians and Americans miss on this
issue regularly, perhaps more than any other single issue.
When you say "yes" or "no", how you say "yes" or "no",
and even what "yes" and "no" mean are very much
culturally determined.

Saying "yes"   Asians say "yes" for a number of reasons. They may say
"yes" to communicate that they are listening. As a normal
part of the pattern of conversation, Japanese will say *hai,
hai, hai,* Malays and Indonesians will say *ya, ya, ya,*
Chinese will say *duay, duay, duay.* This may not mean, "I
agree with what you are saying." It simply may mean, "I
hear what you are saying. I am listening." Americans are
quite likely to interpret a "yes" as acceptance and assume
that agreement has been reached. They are quite
surprised to discover, later on, that the Asian didn't agree
but was merely being a good listener.

Asians may also say "yes" to save face — both their own
and the face of the person with whom they are talking.
A frank discussion of negative topics is considered
impolite and offensive in many Asian countries. An Asian
manager may nod his head and say "yes" to a request
from his boss, even if he disagrees with the request,
because it would be disrespectful to disagree with a
superior. Other times, an Asian manager will respond
with "yes" to a question from an American colleague,
rather than go into the unpleasantness of explaining that
he doesn't understand the question. Americans are likely
to take such a "yes" at face value. They interpret the "yes"
as "I hear you and will comply." Americans, hearing the
words and not reading the context, assume that
something has been accepted or agreed upon, only to
learn later that the Asian was just trying to be polite and
respectful.

Often Americans will hear a "yes" in the flow of conversation, focus on that word or phrase, and assume that agreement has been reached. For Americans, the word "yes" is a very clear statement of agreement or acceptance. Asians, focusing on the context as much as the words, will be able to easily tell the difference between "Yes, I agree with you," and "Yes, I am being polite and listening," when speaking with those from their own culture.

Saying "no"   Asians, of course, do say "no". However, the way they say it is very different from the way Americans communicate disagreement. In Asia, people generally do not want to offend by directly rejecting a person's idea, proposal, or position. Sometimes, Asians will say "no" by saying "yes" and changing the subject. Other times, they will communicate a "no" by using vague statements such as, "I will try," or "Let me think about it," or "It will be difficult." In any case, the Asians with whom they are communicating will have no trouble hearing the "no" implied in these polite messages.

Americans, unless trained to listen for an Asian "no", will often miss the meaning entirely. They are likely to misperceive Asian politeness in saying "yes" as really meaning "yes". Americans, who pay more attention to the words than to the context, expect to hear a very clear and specific "yes" or "no". Being clear on issues of agreement and disagreement allows Americans to know where they stand. Saying "no" is not impolite to an American. Saying "yes" and meaning "no" is.

It becomes extremely important for both Asian and American managers working together to be aware of this area of potential cross-cultural misunderstanding. Just as American managers can benefit from learning what their Asian colleagues are actually communicating when they use the words "yes" and "no", Asian staff can increase their effectiveness and reduce their own frustration by working to make their messages of agreement and disagreement ("yes" and "no") more direct when dealing with their American colleagues.

Being Clear with "Yes" and "No"

1. Say "no" so that an American can hear it. An indirect "no" often is not heard and can lead to misunderstanding and mistrust. Be polite, but clear and direct.
   "I'm sorry, but that will not be possible because . . ."
   "I'm afraid that I cannot do that because . . ."
   "Unfortunately, it cannot be done because . . ."

2. Distinguish between *"Yes, I am listening,"* and *"Yes, I agree,"* or *"Yes, I will do it."*

3. When you are not sure you can do something, you can say "yes" with conditions. It helps the American gain clarity on what will and will not happen.
   "Yes, if . . ."
   "Yes, when . . ."
   "Yes, unless . . ."

4. If you are undecided, let the American know this. Indicating when you will be able to make a decision usually is acceptable.
   "I'll need to check on that. Can I get back to you tomorrow morning?"
   "I will let you know at 3 p.m. today."

"Yes" or "no" questions

Americans often will phrase a question so that it requires a "yes" or "no" answer. "Can you have the order delivered on Wednesday?" rather than "When can the order be delivered?" To an American, having only a "yes" or "no" choice makes the answer clear. Sometimes an American may push for a direct answer, "Give me a simple yes or no. Can you do it by Thursday or not?" To an American, this is a slightly offensive statement, but something that might be said by a boss to a subordinate. Many Asians in this situation may feel pressure to respond with a "yes" out of politeness, even if they really intend a "no". They will certainly feel uncomfortable. In Asia, this type of question is impolite and clearly out of step with the goal of maintaining pleasant, conflict-free communication.

Communicating Understanding

Jerry: "Hey, Chung. Can I ask a favor?"

Chung: (He looks up from his work, turns to Jerry but says nothing.)

Jerry: "We haven't received the estimates for the marketing plan from the L.A. office. They were supposed to have arrived two days ago. I don't know where they are and I need them today."

Chung: (He listens, saying nothing.)

Jerry: "So, can you try to run that down for me?"

Chung: (Chung nods his head.) "I'll try my best."

Jerry: "Call the New York office and ask them to check their computers for whether and when it's been sent."

Chung: (Chung says nothing.)

Jerry: "You got that, Chung?"

Chung: "Yes."

Jerry: "O.K. Thanks. Get it to me as soon as possible." (As Jerry walks away, he wonders, "Did Chung really understand me? Will he do what I asked him to do?")

Feedback to show you understand

All cultures have ways to communicate to the speaker that a message is being received. This is called feedback. As we saw previously, many Asian cultures will say "yes, yes, yes" to convey the message that "I am listening. Please proceed." Japanese also will use a listening noise that sounds something like "mmm .... mmm" to show they are paying attention to the speaker. Alternatively, some Asian cultures believe it is most polite to be quiet while the speaker is talking. Interruption of any sort is considered rude.

Americans give and want a lot of feedback or confirmation that they are being heard. They want to be assured that they are being understood. The typical American conversation is filled with phrases and sounds designed to give feedback that tells the speaker that the listener is, indeed, listening. You can expect to hear lots of comments like, "Yeah", "Okay", "Uh-huh", "Sure", "Uhm hmm", and "I see".

If Americans do not get feedback from others that tells them that the other person is following what they are saying, they may become uncomfortable. They may wonder whether the other person is listening, disagreeing, or just not interested in the conversation. If they do not get enough feedback from the other person, Americans may periodically insert questions into the conversation, e.g. "Do you understand?", "Okay?", "You got that?" They do this to try and get feedback that tells them that they have been understood. If they still do not get a response, Americans may talk more or faster to fill the silence. This, of course, is likely to make their Asian colleagues feel even more uncomfortable.

Communicating understanding non-verbally

Americans also communicate understanding non-verbally. By communicating non-verbally, they let the speaker know they are listening through their gestures and expressions. Americans make eye contact when they begin to speak and periodically throughout the conversation, particularly when they are making a point or want to signal it is the other person's turn to speak.

They nod their heads and smile at appropriate points. When listening, Americans will make more eye contact than when speaking, but will still look away from time to time. When presented with something they don't understand or with which they disagree, Americans often will use facial expressions to communicate that they are confused or upset.

Maintaining eye contact with a superior can be very difficult for many Asians because they have been taught that this is a sign of disrespect. With Americans, not making eye contact does not communicate respect. Instead, it communicates a lack of self-confidence, or worse, that the person may be hiding something.

What This Means For You:

If you are not used to making eye contact when speaking or listening, try to increase your eye contact a little when dealing with Americans. This will communicate self-confidence.

When you don't understand

It is easy to misunderstand Americans. They speak fast. They use a lot of slang. They normally do not have much experience in communicating professionally in a language other than English. They often fail to realize how difficult it is for Asian managers to communicate with them in English. They assume it is easier than it really is.

To the typical American manager, employees who let their supervisors or trainers know when they do not understand something are seen as employees who are doing their best to get the job done right. They are seen as motivated, task-oriented, and open to learning. By not asking, the American manager believes you are creating problems that are bound to surface later. Americans believe that if you act as if you understand when you don't, you will make errors and create problems for yourself and everyone else later.

When you don't understand them, most Americans expect you to stop the conversation and to let them know that you don't understand. For a subordinate to interrupt a superior is rare in Asia. It is not only accepted, but expected in America. It would not be unusual for Americans to politely interrupt their supervisors to be sure they are clearly hearing the message. In American business, it is the employees' responsibility to make sure they clearly understand what is said to them. If they do not understand or are unsure whether or not they have understood a message correctly, they are expected to ask for further explanation or clarification.

Letting someone know you do not understand them is not an easy thing to do, even for Americans. People naturally do not want to appear foolish or ignorant. They don't want to insult their colleagues by suggesting that the information has not been communicated well. They are concerned that even if the information or directions are repeated, they still may not understand. However, in a cross-cultural business environment, it is critical for Asian managers to push themselves to ask for clarification or additional explanation when they do not understand their American colleagues.

Asking for clarification or additional explanation can be very difficult for Asian managers. It goes against the cultural rules they have learned about being a good student and employee. Additionally, Asian managers run the risk of interrupting and asking for explanation too often. If they do, their English competence level will certainly be questioned. However, it is important for Asian managers to check for understanding on those issues of importance. To fail to do so will inevitably lead to miscommunication and mistrust between them and their American counterparts.

What to Do When You're Not Sure You Understand

Here are some techniques you can use to be sure you understand what is communicated to you by your American colleagues. Remember, being open about what you don't know builds trust with Americans. They want to know where you stand.

1. When you don't understand, interrupt early by saying something like:
"Excuse me, but I'm not sure I understand."
"May I ask a question?"
"Can I interrupt? I have a question."
"Could you say that last part again?"

2. Ask for the meaning or an explanation. Be specific about which part of the message you want clarified.
" 'Home run?' What's that?"
"Excuse me, what does 'ambiguous' mean?"
"I understand 'foul ball', but what does 'home run' mean?"

3. Use question words (what, where, when, who, how) to clarify the important parts of the message.
"Where do you want me to send the report?"
"Who are the people you want me to send the memo to?"

4. Try "echoing" — repeat the word or phrase you are not sure you understand or the word(s) that came just before the word you want repeated. Use a questioning tone.
"Ambiguous?"
"Home run?"
"Give the report to Mr. . . .?"

Mr. Roth: *"Mr. Ishida, I've just been called to a special meeting in Osaka . This means that the planning committee meeting scheduled for Friday will have to be changed. Could you please call all the members of the planning group and let them know of this change and see if they can meet next Friday instead?"*

Mr. Ishida: *"Okay, so you want me to let all the members of the*
(his assistant) *planning group know we won't meet on Friday and ask them if they are free to meet the following Friday. Right?"*

To be sure you understand

One of the most valuable skills you can learn to ensure that you really understand the message from another speaker is called summarizing. By this, we mean repeating back, in your own words, the important parts of a message. By confirming the message you have received from the speaker, you not only make sure that you have understood everything correctly, but you help the other person feel confident that you really understood him. This is a skill to employ when the message is important to you and you want to be one hundred percent sure you have understood it.

What This Means For You:

To ensure you understand, summarize what you think you have heard. Repeat back, in your own words, what you believe the speaker means to communicate. Be open to being corrected. You may begin with something like:
  "Right, what you want me to do is . . ."
  "Okay, so you are asking me to . . ."
  "Let me be sure I heard you correctly. You think. . ."
  "So after speaking to Jim, you want me to . . ."

Casual Conversation: Topics to Talk About and Topics to Avoid

John and Bill, two American colleagues, meet in the hallway at work on Monday morning:

Bill: *"Hi, John. How ya doing?"*

John: *"Fine. And you?"*

Bill: *"Great! How was your weekend?"*

John: *"Pretty good. Spent some time with the family on a hike on Saturday and then on Sunday we just did some chores around the house."*

Bill: *"Where did you go hiking?"*

John: *"Near Snow Mountain. There are great hiking trails and fishing streams. And hardly any people. The best part is it's only an hour from the city. Do you like the outdoors?"*

Bill: *"I love to fish, but I don't get to do it as much as I'd like to. I'll have to try your suggestion and go up to Snow Mountain some weekend. Well . . . anyway, got to run. Good speaking to you."*

John: *"Yeah. . . See you again. Take care."*

"Small talk"

With colleagues from work, neighbors, or casual acquaintances, Americans generally go out of their way to be friendly. It may be as simple as "Hi. How's it going?" or "Hi. What's up?", but it conveys the message that "You are in my social network and I want to acknowledge you."

To the verbal American, friendliness also is displayed through casual conversations people have in the halls at work, before a meeting gets down to business, or at the beginning of an appointment. This type of casual conversation is termed "small talk". When Americans make small talk, they talk about anything that provides a common experience — the weather, sports, traffic, their jobs, their families, weekend or vacation activities, movies, or TV. What you talk about usually is not as important as the process of taking a few minutes to "connect" with another person. Small talk helps put people at ease. It communicates that you are a sociable person, interested in others. Because it can serve as the introduction to conversations that are more serious and more important, you often will notice Americans engaging in a few minutes of small talk at the beginning of an American business meeting or appointment, before they get into the substance of the meeting.

How to Make Small Talk with Americans

1. **Make the effort to acknowledge others:**
   Be the first to speak or greet the other person.
   Say "Good morning", "Hello", "Hi".

2. **Talk about topics that are harmless and unlikely to lead to disagreement or strong feelings:**
   Look for things in common: weather, children, sports, work, etc.
   Discuss personal tastes (likes and dislikes) e.g.
   • *"Did you enjoy your Hong Kong vacation?"*
   "What do you think of the food at the new restaurant next door?"

3. **Show that you are listening:**
   Smile, nod your head, look them in the eye.
   React and respond to his or her words.
   Compliment him or her on what they say or do.
   Ask them questions about what they said.

4. **Keep the conversation short.**
   Small talk is only meant to last a few minutes at most.

5. **End the conversation gracefully.**
   Use phrases like:
   "I've got to get back to work. Take care."
   "It's been good talking to you. See you again."

Asians, of course, are very skilled at making casual conversation with people from their own culture. It is when the rules are changed that it becomes difficult. Making small talk American-style, particularly in situations like cocktail parties, can be stressful for those Asian managers who have had little experience with this type of situation. They may not know what to say, how to say it, or to whom they should say it. Asians who are uncomfortable or reluctant to make small talk are seen by Americans as formal, distant, and not very friendly or approachable.

What This Means For You:

You can develop or improve your ability to make small talk. Listen to what Americans talk to each other about and observe how they do it. Push yourself to try this skill. Recognize that initially it may feel uncomfortable, but after practice, it will begin to feel more and more natural.

Personal questions

While Americans ask a lot of questions when conversing with each other, there are some topics they find embarrassing or impolite to discuss in public. Unless you are speaking with a close American friend, you should avoid questions related to:

Money: Financial matters are considered personal. Americans will talk about how much things cost *in general*, but are uncomfortable talking about how much things cost in specific terms. They may offer to tell you the cost of something, but it is best not to ask. Avoid asking questions such as: "How much do you earn?" "How much do you pay for rent?" "How much did that suit cost?"

Appearance:	While Americans often will compliment someone on how well he or she looks ("Your hair looks really pretty fixed like that," or "Looks like you've lost some weight. You look great!"), they normally don't comment or ask questions about weight gained. Americans do not want to be asked a question like, "How much do you weigh?" or hear comments such as, "It looks like you've gained a few kilos."
Age:	Many people, especially women, feel uncomfortable talking about their age. This is slowly changing. However, America's focus on youth makes this a potentially sensitive topic with some people.
Questions about their family status:	Americans love to talk about their families. It won't take much to get them to show you pictures of their children and spouse. At the same time, they resent being asked questions which they feel invade their privacy. For example, such questions as, "Why aren't you married yet?" "When are you going to have another child?" or "Why don't you have children?" are seen as too personal to ask.
Religion:	This is considered to be a private matter. It has the potential to lead to arguments. Most Americans would not ask, "What is your religion?" until they know the other person fairly well.

What This Means For You:

If you are not sure if a question is appropriate to ask, you might say:
"I'd like to ask you a question, but please tell me if it is too personal," or
"I have a question, but I'm not sure whether it's OK to ask in American culture."

Public Presentations

Public presentations, American-style

Americans expect managers to be good communicators. The executive who can speak with confidence and self-assurance in public makes a good impression. Managers who are able to make effective presentations, whether one-on-one to their superiors or in a group meeting, have an advantage, an edge on being promoted, over those who cannot.

Americans like presentations that are short and to the point. Remember, "Time is money." They often state at the beginning of a presentation what it is that they are going to talk about, and conclude by summarizing their major points. In other words, they tell the audience what they are going to say. They say it. They then tell them what they said. They use lots of facts in their arguments, illustrating them with statistics and audio-visual aids (graphs, overheads, slides, etc.). American presenters take pride in appearing to be spontaneous and natural (even though good presenters spend a lot of time preparing beforehand). They like to weave humor, if at all possible, throughout a presentation.

Challenges for the Asian manager

Making public presentations, in English, can be quite difficult for the Asian manager. Apart from the obvious challenge of making a logical and effective presentation in a second language, there are cultural factors at work. From early years, their educational experience has trained Americans, not only to be comfortable expressing their views verbally, but also to be skilled in convincing others. By the time they become executives, Americans usually have had much more practice in delivering public presentations than their Asian counterparts.

Effective Presentations

When you make a presentation, you want your audience to listen to you and to really hear your message. Here are some suggestions on how to make your presentations as effective as possible with an American audience:

Preparation:

1. *Know your subject.*
   Be comfortable with all aspects of the topic so you are ready to respond to questions or comments.

2. *Know your audience.*
   What is their background, expertise, expectations?

3. *Limit the content of your presentation.*
   It is better to say less effectively and have it remembered or acted on.

4. *Rehearse.*
   Practice your comments out loud to a friend, in front of a mirror, or into a tape recorder so you become comfortable with the words, pacing, and tone of your presentation.

5. *Use notes, an outline or key phrases to assist your memory.*
   Do not read from a page. Avoid word for word preparation.

Delivery:

1. *Make eye contact.*
   Pick out one person or a group of people in a part of the room and deliver a few of your remarks to them. Then switch to another part of the audience.

2. *Talk naturally and make sure you are loud enough.*
   Vary your speaking pattern and tone. Slow down and gesture to make important points. Pause before and after key points.

3. *The first and last words are the most important.*
   The first create the atmosphere and the last leave your listeners with your message.

4. *Use audio-visual aids.*
   Slides, overheads, charts, graphs, videos, etc. give life to your message and take the focus off you directly. Prepare and practice with A-V equipment before the presentation.

5. *Be enthusiastic about your message.*
   Enthusiasm is contagious.

6. *Expect to be nervous.*
   It is not unusual. Remind yourself that you are prepared and can cope. Act confident, even if you are not.

Paying attention: Different rules, different glasses

Sometimes, in the middle of a presentation, training session, or business meeting, an Asian manager will turn to a neighbor to ask for a translation or clarification of what the speaker said. For many Asians, this is the polite and expected way to get help. In America, when a speaker is talking to a group, it is considered impolite not to give your full attention to the speaker. If you need help understanding a point made, the American expects you to ask the speaker. After all, the American reasons, if one person doesn't understand, then probably there are others as well who don't understand. Americans regularly misinterpret side conversations by Asians as expressions of disinterest or rudeness. Different cultural rules and glasses are at work here.

What This Means For You:

When attending a presentation, meeting or training session conducted by an American, try to minimize "side conversations". If you work with Americans who get annoyed by such conversations, help them to understand what is really going on.

11
Business and Social Etiquette

An Asian manager recounts his experience of visiting his American boss' home for dinner:
"It was really quite strange. When I first arrived, they greeted me and then asked me if I would like a tour of the house. What could I say? We went through the whole house, even the bathrooms and the kitchen!! They opened the gift I brought right in front of all the other guests. At dinner, after I was through with my first serving of food, they asked if I would like more. Of course, I said 'No,' not wanting them to think I was impolite. They never asked again!! It is very strange to visit Americans in their homes."

Etiquette allows people to interact smoothly

Social manners, customs, and etiquette are the tip of the iceberg we have called culture. The social rituals, customs and formalities, the do's and don'ts, are the first and most obvious things we notice when we go to a new country or meet someone who comes from a different culture. They are behaviors that are generally expected in specific, social situations. For example, while Japanese businessmen bow at their first meeting, their American counterparts are likely to shake hands.

How we are greeted, what others call us, even how close to us they stand, all contribute to the first impressions that encourage us either to get to know another person better or to limit our contact. If we feel uncomfortable at this point, we may never go further. Social etiquette provides the "social oil" that allows relationships to flow smoothly from an initial to ongoing basis. If you are working with those of another culture, understanding and being comfortable with the social etiquette of that culture is necessary for your success.

Asians value etiquette

For the vast majority of Asians, social etiquette is extremely important. There is a deeply-rooted tradition of paying attention to and respecting manners throughout Asia. How to talk to someone, how to present yourself, how to be a good host and good guest are issues to which Asians give a lot of attention. How you behave reflects upon your character, your family, and your company.

Americans and social etiquette

Americans are also concerned about proper social etiquette and being polite. They have very clear rules for a wide range of social behavior. However, because of the important values of individuality and informality, they also allow greater freedom in certain situations and do not always follow the accepted social etiquette rules.

When in the United States, Americans will expect you to follow American social etiquette. (Remember, many Americans will see you as an "odd" American, on the way to becoming just like them.) Americans, like Asians, do not expect foreigners to be completely familiar with their ways. For example, when dining, they do not expect Asians to know a white wine glass from a red wine glass, which fork is the salad fork and which is for the main course. If they believe the foreigner is trying to be polite and not give offense, Americans, like Asians, usually will be forgiving if their customs are not followed. However, there are some types of social behavior that are considered unacceptable to most Americans. Behaviors like cutting in line, not treating service people (taxi drivers, waitresses, etc.) with "proper" respect, smoking in non-smoking areas, almost always will offend and provoke a strong negative reaction.

The challenge for Asian managers wanting to be polite is to figure out which are the important social rules they must follow and which are the ones they may or may not follow, depending on their inclination or comfort level. Clearly, the same challenge exists for Americans wanting to interact effectively with Asians.

The following are some of the social etiquette expectations in American culture. Some style-switching of customs and manners is easy. Other changes are far more difficult because they touch upon ways of behaving that just come naturally. It is important to remember that differences in social etiquette and customs, just like everything else we have discussed in this book, are neither "right" nor "wrong", but rather different from what you are used to. The goal in presenting these topics, as with the rest of the book, is to decrease your frustration by giving you information on American cultural rules and glasses and to increase your potential effectiveness by indicating places where style-switching may be to your benefit.

Meeting and Getting to Know Americans

Business cards

Americans exchange business cards with colleagues, but with far less frequency and with far less formality than their Asian colleagues. They make the exchange, not necessarily at the moment of meeting, but when they decide they may want to be in contact with each other again. Business cards generally are not exchanged in social, out-of-work, settings unless specifically requested. Most Americans are aware of the importance of business cards in the Asian work setting. The first (and sometimes the only) piece of advice Americans visiting Asia are likely to get is how to prepare and present their business card.

Shaking hands

It is not always clear when to shake hands with Americans. In business situations, men and women normally shake hands when they first meet. They also usually will shake hands at the end of a formal meeting. They may or may not shake hands at subsequent meetings. Secretaries are introduced to office visitors and are prepared to shake hands, if a hand is extended by the visitor.

When Americans shake hands, they usually do so for just a few seconds, looking each other in the eye and smiling. When they shake, they grasp the other's hand firmly, not loosely, moving it up and down two or three times. Generally, Americans like a firm handshake. They see a weak handshake as a sign of weak character.

Forms of address

It is common for many people in the United States to use first names in most business situations. Many employees will even call their boss by his or her first name. This is not considered rude. Many American bosses prefer it.

When Americans first meet, to introduce someone, they may use, "Mr.", "Mrs.", "Miss", or, more recently, "Ms."

(Pronounced "Miz", it refers to a married or unmarried woman. This is always safe to use.) They typically would make an introduction by saying something like, "John, I'd like you to meet Ms. Washington of XYZ Company. She's here to meet with the Sales Department today." Ms. Washington would typically say , "Call me Betty." The relationship would be on a first name basis from there on.

If people are very senior in age or rank or if the situation is very formal (for example, giving a speech), then the more formal term of address may be used. For superiors, it is safest initially to use "Mr." or "Ms." until they let you know otherwise. If you are uncomfortable calling your boss by a first name, you need not change your behavior. Americans will be somewhat amused by your formality, but not offended.

Nicknames

Americans often have difficulty pronouncing and remembering Asian names. They are likely to give you a "nickname", as they do to many of their American colleagues. Nicknames are familiar or descriptive names that are used in everyday conversation. They may be your initials ("J.W."), a shortened version of your name ("Ed" for Edward), or just a familiar name that seems to fit. If your name is hard for Americans to remember or pronounce, you may want to come up with an easier one for yourself.

Ritual conversation: Greetings, goodbyes, and other commonly used phrases

When American acquaintances such as office colleagues greet each other, they typically say things like, "How's it going?" or "What's happening?" or "What's up?" These are ritual phrases that do not require any response other than "Fine, and you?" or "Not much. What's up with you?"

Like every language, American English is filled with phrases designed to make interactions easy and flowing. Statements such as, "Let's get together some time," "See you later," "We'll have to have lunch together," are not to be taken seriously. They are a form of social communication that allows for smooth and comfortable endings of conversations.

"Excuse me"

Asians often notice that there are two phrases which Americans say quite often: "Excuse me," and "Thank you." It seems that Americans are always using these ritual words. "Excuse me" relates to Americans' sense of personal privacy and personal space. If they get physically too close, for example, accidentally touching someone in a crowded elevator or bumping into someone on a crowded street, they will say, "Excuse me." They are apologizing for getting closer than is culturally acceptable and comfortable and to indicate their action was not intentional.

Americans also will say, "Excuse me," when they disturb someone's psychological privacy. They will say, "Excuse me," when they want to ask a question ("Excuse me, could you tell me how to get to . . . "). They use it when interrupting a conversation, or when they make involuntary body noises (burps, yawns, sneezes) which they believe are impolite and disturbing to others.

"Thank you"

Asians also note that Americans say "thank you" often. It is a ritual, polite statement that is a regular part of every well-mannered American's daily vocabulary. It is applied to anyone who provides you a service, irrespective of whether or not doing so is part of their job. Americans will say "thank you" to waitresses who bring them a cup of coffee as well as the office cleaning lady who empties their trash.

Americans also may say "thank you" to decrease their sense of obligation. They don't like to be in debt in interpersonal relations. In many cases, a sincere "thank you" is all that is required to clear a debt of personal obligation between two Americans. To Asians, this may seem very strange indeed, for how can you repay a debt merely by saying "thank you"?

Eye contact

For many Asians, direct eye contact can be perceived as

a challenge. They often avoid eye contact with superiors to communicate respect. Americans may interpret this behavior to mean either that the person is hiding something, not being honest, or that the person lacks confidence. To an American, what is considered to be appropriate eye contact during conversation is sustained eye contact which lasts for five to seven seconds, with periodic breaks of two to three seconds in between. People who maintain this level of eye contact are seen as interested, sincere, and confident.

Telephone etiquette

Often, your first (and sometimes only) meeting with someone is over the telephone. How you present yourself and how you respond can be critical to making a good impression. Here are some tips for telephone etiquette that can make your phone contacts positive for you and your company when dealing with Americans:

1) Respond promptly. Don't let the phone ring more than two or three times.

2) Answer with your name and organization/department if the call is not coming through your secretary. ("Hello, C.K. Huang, Accounting Department.")

3) Don't leave people on hold for more than a minute. Explain delays. If you need more time to get the information, let the caller know and ask if they prefer to hold or prefer that you call them back.

4) Return phone calls or phone messages within 24 hours.

5) If you are making a call and need more than one or two minutes of the other person's time, it is polite to inquire, "Are you free to talk now?" If not, they can suggest a time to call you back or suggest a time for you to call them again.

6) Don't remain silent while the other person continues to speak. Respond with words or vocalizations like "uh-huh", "I see", "yes", "go on", to let the speaker know you are involved and listening.

7)   Get to the point quickly and be brief.

8)   If you know you need to have a long conversation, set up a telephone appointment in advance. This way the person you are calling can set aside enough time to talk without interruptions.

9)   For international calls made to people at their homes, try to respect personal privacy and family time by calling no later than 9 p.m. and no earlier than 7 a.m. U.S. time, if at all possible.

10) End the conversation on a positive note ("Thanks for your help." "Give my regards to Jim.") and a summary of what was discussed or agreed upon, if appropriate.

What This Means For You:

If you are unsure as to what is the most appropriate response in a social situation, it is safest to respond with typical Asian formality. Americans may view your response with some amusement, but you will never make the mistake of being too casual at the wrong time.

Business Entertaining and Socializing

Invitations

Americans will often end a conversation with a general invitation such as, "We'll have to get together again soon." Or, "Let's have lunch together sometime." What they mean to say by these words is that they enjoyed talking with you or that they like you well enough to have lunch with you. However, these are not real invitations. If it is a real invitation, Americans will set a definite date. They might say, "Are you free for lunch next Tuesday?" Or, "I'll call you tonight so we can set a date," and they will call you. If you are not sure whether the invitation is sincere or just the American being polite, it is appropriate to ask, "Would you like to set a date now to get together or would you rather wait?"

Americans usually are very clear about accepting or declining invitations. They will say, "Yes. I'd love to come." Or, "I'm sorry, but I have other plans for Saturday." When Americans are unsure, they might say, "I'll have to check my calendar to see what plans I have for Saturday. Can I get back to you tomorrow?" Once again, Americans prefer a clear, direct response that lets them know where they stand.

If you set a date to meet, go to lunch, or visit an American's home, and you are unable to attend, it is important to let your host know as soon as possible. It is considered extremely rude to say you are coming and to not show up. Be sure to phone your regrets as far in advance as possible. The host may want to invite someone else or change the date of the event to suit your schedule. In more formal situations, where there is an invitation card, you may notice the words, "RSVP" or "Please Reply" at the bottom of the card. This is a request to let the host (or sponsor) of the event know whether or not you will be attending. Sometimes, an invitation will say "Regrets only", meaning a reply is requested only if you are not coming.

*Time to
arrive/time
to leave*

Business Appointments: If an appointment has been made far in advance, it is a good idea to call to confirm it. Arrive five to ten minutes early for business appointments. This shows respect for your host's time. (Remember how important efficient use of time is to the typical American executive.) Keep to the time you have scheduled to meet or ask, "How much time will we have to meet today?"

*Business breakfasts,
lunches, and dinners:* Americans conduct a lot of business over food. They typically have business breakfasts and lunches at restaurants where appropriate and are expected to discuss business topics during the meal. Much business entertaining is conducted over dinner at restaurants as well. It is not unusual to mix business and social topics at one time. It is appropriate to arrive on time for business breakfasts, lunches, and dinners. Breakfasts can be quite early (7-9 a.m.) as Americans want to get as much as possible done each day. Business dinners usually begin between 7-8 p.m. and will typically last for one and a half to two hours.

*Open houses,
receptions, and
cocktail parties:* Invitations to such events normally comes with a time range. For example, a cocktail party may be held from 6-8 p.m. It is acceptable to come and go any time within that period.

As a guest at a private home:

Dinner parties in an American's home usually begin around 7 p.m. and can end as early as 10 p.m. or as late as midnight. Try to arrive five to fifteen minutes after the invited time. If you are going to be more than twenty minutes late, it is polite to call and let the host or hostess know when you expect to arrive. The time to leave is somewhat open, but it is expected you will stay after dinner is served, for coffee and conversation. Take your cues from Americans present as to the appropriate time to leave. Once one or two of them get ready to leave, you can join them to make your exit, if you wish. Try not to be the last person to leave. Your hosts may be more tired than they look!

Gifts

There are few specific rules on gift-giving, but there are some general customs which Americans follow. On the whole, they give fewer gifts than Asians and most of those go to close friends and relatives. They do not always reciprocate gift-giving. Do not be insulted if you give a gift and receive nothing in return.

When Americans are invited to someone's home, they will usually bring a present. For example, a bottle of wine, flowers or candy is appropriate. Sometimes, bosses will give a gift to their secretary if they have been away on a long trip, on the secretary's birthday, or as an expression of thanks for special efforts. The gift is for her and, even if it is something like chocolates, it may or may not be shared with other office colleagues. If you are visiting America and wish to express thanks to a host or hostess, a small inexpensive gift from your home country would be most welcome.

In giving gifts to Americans, you will notice that they may open them right away, in front of you. They usually will express their appreciation, by saying "Thank you", or writing you a follow-up note of appreciation. While Asians may view the exchange of gifts as a way of fine tuning ongoing relationships, Americans tend to be less concerned about exchanging gifts. They may give a gift spontaneously to a friend or a colleague just because they saw something the other person would like, expecting no gift or obligation in return.

American businesspeople sometimes give gifts which are advertisements of one sort or another (i.e. desk calendars, pens, or calculators with corporate logos). These are usually not expensive gifts. In Asia, gifts take on a much greater meaning. Gifts cement the relationship between business partners. In the U.S., businesspeople are somewhat suspicious of gifts. They reason since you don't need a close relationship to do business in America, then you don't need a regular exchange of gifts. The contract will do just fine. In fact, valuable gifts may be seen as an embarrassing attempt at bribery. Therefore, Americans may be reluctant to give or to accept personal gifts from people who are in a position to grant or to receive favors. Many American companies have clear policies prohibiting the giving and the receiving of gifts beyond a certain value. It is important for the Asian manager to be aware that such restrictions exist so as to prevent embarrassment and misunderstanding.

The cocktail party

The cocktail party is a unique American institution. Its goal is to provide an opportunity for people to meet and talk to others — lots of them! Therefore, Americans move around a great deal at cocktail parties. They do what is termed "networking" — meeting and getting to know (at least on a superficial level) potential business contacts.

The basic rule of a cocktail party is to pick out people who look interesting to you and to talk to them. Anyone can talk to anyone else. It is quite acceptable to join a group or to walk up to another individual and introduce yourself. The discussion tends to be relatively light. People make small talk, focusing on issues people have in common (family, vacations, sports) or topical events (politics, business).

Many Asians feel distinctly uncomfortable at American-style cocktail parties. The cocktail party can seem too short, with much less to eat and drink than would be provided at an Asian social gathering. In addition to requiring great fluency in English, it also requires participants to be social "self-starters", introducing themselves to others and having numbers of conversations one-on-one at a superficial level. Generally, Asians prefer social gatherings in which everyone knows everyone else and where everyone joins in the fun of group activities.

Meeting and Getting to Know Americans

Whether at a cocktail party or at work, you will find American colleagues open to meeting and getting to know you, at least on a superficial level. The following guidelines are principles that Americans use which can help you to improve your conversational skills and to build relationships with Americans.

1. **If it is a first meeting, introduce yourself.**
    Don't wait to be presented. ("Hi, My name is Abdul Rahman.") Smile and look the person in the eye when you are first introduced.

2. **Start conversations.**
    Don't wait for the other person to begin speaking first. Be the first to say "Hello."

3. **Make it personal and positive.**
    Use the person's name in your conversation. Compliment him or her for good ideas, good questions, or things accomplished.

4.   **Ask questions that go somewhere.**
    Ask for their feelings or thoughts on an issue.
    Stay away from questions that require a short
    "yes" or "no" answer. Questions that begin
    with what, how, or why tend to get longer
    answers. (For example, "What do you think
    about . . .?)

5.   **Help keep the conversation going.**
    Share your feelings and thoughts so the
    listener will know your opinions. Let the
    speaker know you are really interested by
    your non-verbal reactions (head nods, smiles,
    "uh-huh", when appropriate) and by
    responding to his or her words.

*Paying
your share*

If you are invited to lunch or dinner in America, it is
expected, as in Asia, that the person who extends the
invitation is the one who will pay the bill. When office
colleagues or friends go out to eat, however, Americans
usually expect that each person will pay his or her share.
The concept of "you pay this time, I'll pay next time," is
not nearly as common among Americans as it is among
Asian friends or colleagues.

*Drinking
alcohol*

Drinking patterns vary greatly among Americans. Some
people never drink alcohol (beer, wine, whisky). Others
drink occasionally on weekends or at cocktail parties. Yet
others will have drinks before dinner, wine with a meal,
or go out to a bar with friends. All are acceptable
patterns. What generally is not acceptable, however, is
for the American executive to drink excessively in the
company of work colleagues. Being drunk in public is
not looked upon favorably.

For the Asian manager visiting the United States, it is
important to know that it is acceptable not to drink
alcohol when others around you are drinking. Having a
soft (non-alcoholic) drink is a reasonable alternative to

drinking alcohol, if you so desire. If you do drink, you need to be very careful about driving. Never drive in the U.S. after you have had two or more alcoholic drinks. Penalties for driving under the influence of alcohol are severe and they are enforced.

How You Can Offend or Be Offended Unintentionally

Americans at work, regardless of their status, usually go out of their way to make the workplace pleasant and conflict-free. Work colleagues generally treat each other with politeness and respect and are most comfortable when the work environment feels friendly. Sometimes, it is possible to offend without meaning to. Even though your intentions are positive, your actions may communicate quite a different message to someone wearing different cultural glasses. What may be offensive in one culture, may have no meaning, positive or negative, in another. Presented below are some of the ways we can offend each other, without the slightest intention of doing so.

Smoking

In the last ten years or so in American society, there has been an increasing level of concern about and sensitivity to the effects of smoking cigarettes. Many Americans who previously smoked have given it up. Smoking is banned in many public buildings, on internal American airline flights, and in many businesses. Restaurants, if they allow smoking at all, have smoking and non-smoking sections.

In America, either at work or out of work, you should not light up a cigarette without first asking, "Do you mind if I smoke?" Don't be surprised if people respond by saying they would rather you didn't smoke. When visiting America, if you wish to smoke, pay careful attention to whether or not you are in an environment where smoking is allowed. In Asia, although not expected, it would be considered polite at a business meeting with Americans to inquire if anyone objects to you smoking.

Taking your turn

When Americans are in a situation where numbers of people are waiting to be served, for instance, in a line in a bank or a queue at a bus stop, they are very careful to follow the rule of "wait your turn". Reflecting the value of equality in American society, no one in a public situation gets preference over anyone else. The person who arrives first, gets served first. If you break this social rule, you are likely to get rude stares and perhaps a comment such as, "Hey buddy, I was here first," to remind you to take your place at the end of the line.

American non-verbal behavior that can offend Asians

Non-verbal behavior includes all the ways we communicate with each other over and above the words we speak. The way we communicate with our hands, face and other parts of our body, for example, as well as appropriate space and distance between people, are all part of non-verbal behavior. Often, the non-verbal behavior of another culture does not fit with what you expect or what you are used to seeing and doing yourself.

There is a whole range of non-verbal gestures that Americans typically find acceptable that can cause offense or discomfort to Asians. These range from passing and receiving things with the left hand, to showing the bottom (soles) of your feet to someone, to calling someone to come to you with upturned fingers, palm facing the body or with just one finger. These, and others like them, are specific gestures that Americans visiting or working in Asia can and should learn to eliminate. The American in the U.S.A. or the short-term visitor to Asia would probably have no idea that these behaviors can cause offense.

When Americans communicate at work, they tend to use more hand and arm motions than is customary for many Asians. Sometimes, this can be distracting for their Asian co-workers. Americans touch colleagues, both male and female, more often and in different ways, than is acceptable in Asian countries. While same-sex touching is more acceptable in many Asian societies than in America, it is not unusual for an American man to slap a male colleague on the back or to squeeze his shoulder.

It would not be unusual for a male American boss to touch his secretary on the shoulder if she is seated and he is standing beside or behind her, bending forward describing work to be done. While this is now less and less common due to increasing concerns related to sexual harassment issues, it is not impossible that an American boss might give a hug of greeting to his secretary upon his return from a lengthy trip abroad. These behaviors can be extremely unsettling if you are not prepared for them or you may misinterpret them as having a sexual meaning. If you are uncomfortable with this type of touching, it is always acceptable to let the American know this. This should be sufficient to stop the behavior.

Asian non-verbal behavior that can offend Americans

The diversity of Asian cultures makes it difficult to point to specific non-verbal behaviors of Asians that regularly produce discomfort for Americans. Some Asian cultures have different rules about spitting, blowing your nose, littering, staring, even belching after a meal, that are quite different from what is perceived as "good manners" by Americans. When visiting the U.S. or entertaining American guests, learn about and pay attention to these differences in what is considered socially acceptable and appropriate.

One classic cross-cultural "miss" (misunderstanding) revolves around the issue of smiling. Americans smile often, but usually as a reaction to good news or happy feelings. They generally do not smile when embarrassed or anxious as do Asians. An American would not deliver bad news with a smile. Asians, on the other hand, smile for good and bad news, to express positive as well as to cover up negative emotions. When Asians smile in situations where Americans would not, Americans often misinterpret the smile or laugh, wondering, "He just failed his examination. Why is he smiling? He must not take any of this seriously." Americans would expect someone in this situation to show disappointment or regret. This misinterpretation of the Asian's reaction to embarrassment can result in Americans feeling angry, frustrated or confused because the response (smiling, laughing) is the opposite response of what they are expecting. While Asians will not be able to change this deeply-held cultural response easily, it is important to be aware that it holds high potential to be misunderstood by culturally-unaware Americans.

Another way Asians can unintentionally offend American office colleagues is by speaking in their native language in the presence of an American who is not fluent in their language. While the ideal is that each American who goes overseas should be fluent in the language of the host country, the reality is far from this. If you are fluent in English, Americans often, mistakenly, assume that when you are speaking in a language they don't understand, you are discussing something you don't want to share with them. They may think that you are purposely trying to exclude them, rather than understanding that you are just more comfortable speaking in your own language. They can feel left out and may interpret your behavior as being rude and inconsiderate.

What This Means For You:

If you are in a situation where it would be more effective to carry on a conversation in your own language, explain to the American the reason for this. You might say something like, "I can explain this concept to Abdul Aziz better in Malay. Excuse me for a minute."

Section IV:
Making Cultural
Differences Work
for You

12
Cross-Cultural Skills for the Global Manager

Style-Switching at Work

When you learn a new language, rather than lose or forget your native tongue, you become better able to speak with a greater number of people in ways they find more comfortable and acceptable. You do not become a dramatically different person, only a more effective communicator. Likewise, when you gain knowledge and skills in dealing with people from another culture, you do not become a different person. You become better able to communicate with and to understand a greater number of people.

Learning about a new culture, like learning a new language, gives you a new set of skills. It helps you to get your needs met in ways that are acceptable and understandable to someone from another culture. Learning about another culture also teaches you about yourself and your society.

In learning to cross cultures, it is not expected (and probably not possible) for you to change your cultural identity. You have to be true to yourself. It is absolutely appropriate to value and to follow your own ways.

However, you can style-switch selectively, choosing those actions which are likely to provide you with the greatest gains. The key is to adapt to specific parts of another culture that will make your work life easier and more productive. What you choose to adopt ultimately must be comfortable for you.

Rules for Style-Switching

Changing behavior is hard under any circumstance. Changing behavior in a cross-cultural environment, whether it be learning to say "no" directly, speaking up in meetings, or telling the boss bad news, can be even more challenging. To maximize your chances of successfully making a change:

1. **Be selective.**
   Look for behavior that, if modified, will make a real difference for you at work.

2. **Do not go too far or too fast in making changes.**
   Initially, pick one or two behaviors that you think you can change. Don't try to make too many changes at one time.

3. **Practice.**
   Rehearse the new behavior by yourself or with a friend before trying it out in the actual situation.

4. **Pick your timing, pick your audience.**
   Try out new behavior at low risk times, with low risk people, to gain practice and confidence in the new behavior.

5. Remember that **any change**, especially changes in behavior our culture has taught us is "normal", **will feel uncomfortable at first.** Only after you have practiced a new behavior for a while will you begin to feel comfortable and natural using it.

Your Role as a Cross-Cultural Guide

*Your role
as a bridge
across
cultures*

If you are a manager in an American multinational company, you have a unique role to play. Whether you want it or not, you are in the special position of cross-cultural guide or translator. Your American colleagues need your insight and assistance in making sense out of the business environment, the government, and the workforce they may employ. At the same time, the people you supervise, office colleagues, business contractors, customers, and many others who may not speak English or who may have limited exposure to American culture, need your help in interpreting the strange and often confusing behavior of the American manager and the corporate culture he or she represents. You are in the middle. You are uniquely able to help people from different cultures understand and work effectively with each other. If you are a manager experienced in working with foreigners, you probably already do this. We suggest that you continue with it, perhaps even more consciously. If you are new to working with foreigners, we suggest mentally adding this to your job description. Being a cross-cultural guide is a critical role that can affect the success or failure of a multinational business venture.

How to be a Cross-Cultural Guide

Depending on your relationship (boss, colleague, subordinate) with the American manager, you have a number of possible roles you can play to assist him or her in understanding and responding appropriately to cross-cultural differences at work. Here are some behaviors that you can employ to help an American manager become more effective in your culture.

---

1. **Explain your culture's point of view.**
   Be a cultural interpreter, sharing the logic and sense behind why people act they way they do. You have critical cultural information that your American colleague may not know. *("In my culture . . .")*

2. **Teach through questions.**
   Ask questions that get Americans to realize that there are alternative explanations for behavior or ways of looking at the world. *("How do they do . . . . in American culture?" "What do Americans think about . . .?")*

3. **Anticipate problems.**
   You may see issues coming that go unnoticed by your American colleagues. Look ahead and alert them to unforeseen surprises.

4. **Present ideas/ask questions** that raise issues which the American manager may not have considered. Help Americans learn the questions to ask. Some of the factors which are important in your culture may not be predictable from the American cultural perspective.

5. **Remind Americans** of the importance of paying attention to cultural rules and glasses by pointing out how traditional Asian beliefs, values, and customs are part of the everyday fabric of doing business in Asia.

How to Get Out of Difficult Situations and How to Prevent Yourself from Getting Into Them

The most critical variable in working effectively with someone from a different culture is goodwill. The intention or desire to work together is the strongest bridge across cultural differences. All sorts of cross-cultural miscommunications and misperceptions can be excused if the basic desire to understand and communicate is there.

However, goodwill is not always enough. Cross-cultural missing (misunderstanding) can and does occur even among co-workers who have the best of intentions. In order for you to be effective cross-culturally, you need to know how to get out of difficult cross-cultural situations and what to do when you don't know how to act.

Take time to diagnose when cross-cultural misses occur

When a cross-cultural misunderstanding occurs, you will know it because you will end up feeling frustrated, annoyed, confused, or embarrassed. When these feelings arise in a cross-cultural situation, use them as a cue to tell you that it is time to step back to try to understand what happened and why. If you don't diagnose and understand, you inevitably will experience those same unsettling feelings again and again. You need to ask yourself if this is a problem that comes from cross-cultural differences in looking at and responding to the world, or differences in personalities, expectations, or expertise. Is this typical American behavior or just the way this one person acts? Then, you have to figure out what you can do to avoid this problem in the future.

One helpful technique for diagnosing a problem is to review it in your mind like you might replay a videotape in slow motion. This way you can really see what is going on. If you "replay" (review) enough cross-cultural misses, you will begin to see patterns of behavior that repeatedly cause problems. You will become better at anticipating these cross-cultural misunderstandings. With time and practice, this will help you to prevent them from occurring.

Our interpretation of events determines our reactions

When you replay the cross-cultural interaction, focus on what happened and your reaction. We normally think that our reaction, either our feelings or how we respond, follows immediately after an event or behavior. Consider the following situation: Your American boss asks you to work late on a night when you have an important family commitment. Feeling that you cannot refuse your boss, you agree to stay, but you feel upset. It may look something like this:

BEHAVIOR ⟶ REACTION
(What happened)   (Your feelings and response)

Your boss made a request for you to stay late (behavior) and you said "yes", but felt angry (reaction). However, we know it is not quite that simple. In reality, we see behavior through our cultural glasses and we respond or react according to our cultural rules. More accurately, the interaction looks like this:

BEHAVIOR ⟶ INTERPRETATION ⟶ REACTION
(What happened)   (Your culture's rules   (Your feelings
                  and glasses)   and response)

Your interpretation, how you see your boss' behavior and the request to work late, will provide you with directions on the best way to respond to this behavior. Much of our interpretation — how we see things and how we should respond, comes from our culture. If you see your boss as being demanding, inflexible, or uncaring about your feelings or your situation, you may respond in one way (stay, but feel upset because you believe you have no choice). If, however, you see your boss as not intending to put you in a difficult situation, but just following American cultural rules (that is, expecting you to say "no" if you cannot do it), you may not like the request, but you may respond quite differently. You certainly will feel different towards your boss, even if you don't respond any differently at all.

Steps in diagnosing cross-cultural missing

Therefore, to understand a situation in which a cross-cultural misunderstanding has occurred and in order to respond appropriately, you need to take time out to break the process down and to analyze it. Ask yourself three separate sets of questions:

1) "What happened?" "What am I seeing?" "What am I hearing?"
  (Describe the situation objectively without any evaluation of it being good or bad, right or wrong.)

2) "What does this behavior mean in my culture?" and "What might this mean in American culture?"
  (Interpret the behavior through your own and through American cultural glasses, if you can.)

3) "What's the best way to respond?" or "How can I find out the most appropriate way to respond?"

In short, the best way to prevent or to get out of any cross-cultural dilemma in which you may find yourself is to think ahead or review what had occurred or what may occur, analyze the situation from the American as well as from your own cultural perspective, and try to find a win-win approach that will meet your needs as well as those of your American colleagues.

Ask culture learning questions

Sometimes when solving these types of problems, a lack of information on how Americans think and respond can be a stumbling block. Books like this one can help. You also need to be comfortable with, and develop skills in, asking culture learning questions. Culture learning questions are questions you ask Americans which give you information about what Americans usually do or say in specific situations.

Americans, like Asians, are happy to respond to questions about their culture, especially if these questions are asked in a non-judgemental, non-evaluating way. If you ask questions such as,

"What do Americans think about . . . .?"

"Is it O.K. to say . . . .?"

"What's the best way to respond when an American . . .?"

you usually will get not only a positive response from the typical American, but also valuable cultural information that can help you anticipate likely behaviors or reactions. Culture learning questions are great topics for small talk or dinner table conversation.

Find a cross-cultural guide

While we have suggested that you become a cross-cultural guide for both your American colleagues and those of your own culture who have not had much exposure to different cultures, it is equally important that you find a cross-cultural guide for yourself. Ideally, this should be a person whom you neither supervise nor who supervises you. This person can be an American or can be someone from your own country who has more cross-cultural experience than you. This person should be someone whom you can go to periodically for advice when things happen that you don't understand. You should be able to ask questions like, "Something happened yesterday and I'm confused. Can you tell me what you think was going on and what is the best way for me to respond?" All of us need to have cross-cultural guides or teachers as well as to be cross-cultural guides ourselves.

Learn about American culture

To prevent problems if you are working with Americans, become a student of America and Americans. Americans are proud of their culture and will appreciate your interest. Make it your job to learn more about the culture of the people with whom you work. One way of learning more about American culture is to study it. In addition to asking culture learning questions, become an observer of how Americans act with each other and with Asians. Notice what Americans say and do (and how they say and do it) when they are at a business meeting, at a cocktail party, or greeting each other in the hallway. Watch American movies and television. They reflect American values and beliefs. Read American magazines, books and newspapers. Note what the subjects are, what people are concerned with, how they express themselves. (See page 243 for recommended readings on learning more about American culture.)

While learning about American culture, remember you are learning about generalizations, which may or may not be true for any one individual. Never lose sight of the importance of responding to each person as an individual with a unique personality, life history, competencies, interests, and expectations. Keep in mind the great variation among Americans, depending upon economic status, sex, race, part of the country from which they come, and how long they have been in America. Cross-cultural generalizations are hypotheses or best guesses that you need to check out with each individual and with each situation you encounter.

Learn about your own culture

By interacting with others, you inevitably learn more about yourself. By working with someone from another culture, you cannot help but learn more about your own culture. To make working relations with someone from a different culture easier and more productive, learn more about your own culture's beliefs, values, and rules of behavior. Learning about your own culture helps you to understand how it affects your motivation, behavior, and thoughts. Challenge the natural tendency to see your culture's way as the "right" or "normal" way to look at the world. While there is nothing wrong with liking or preferring the way your culture does something, you need to be careful that your own cultural glasses don't blind you to accepting and working with other ways of looking at and responding to the world.

Cross-cultural understanding makes you less frustrated and more effective

When you have a cross-cultural misunderstanding, slowing down the process and examining the cultural rules and glasses, both your own and those of the American, will take some of the frustration out of the interaction. You will regain a sense of control. It helps you to be less judgmental and to feel less negative if you can see that your frustration is coming from a predictable cultural difference. More importantly, it gives you the freedom to change your reaction or behavior if you wish. In this way, you can be more effective and interact more positively with American (and other culturally-different) colleagues in the future.

A Final Word

*Many ways
of achieving
the same
goal*

This book has covered a lot of ground in exploring problem prevention or troubleshooting to decrease your frustrations when interacting with Americans. However, cross-cultural differences are more than a source of frustration. They are an opportunity to find different, and often better, ways of getting the job done. As we have mentioned previously, no one culture has a monopoly on the "best" way. There are many ways of achieving the same end, all of which can be fruitful. Having an increased ability to appreciate and to work with people from different cultures can enrich and make our lives more productive.

*Americans
have much
to learn
from Asians*

Americans have much to learn from Asian cultures which have proven to be dynamic and successful over many centuries. As American/business re-evaluates management values and behavior that work in a changing world of global economies, shifting markets, and ever-increasing demands for flexibility, they can benefit from examining some of the core business values and behaviors that have served Asian societies so well for so long. In particular, Americans in business and their companies may find value in the Asian emphasis on interdependence and teamwork, on taking the long-term perspective, on emphasizing the importance of developing relationships that go beyond any one contract or business deal, on emphasizing cooperation and agreement management over competition and conflict resolution, and on balancing the head with the heart, by combining facts and logic with a concern for the welfare of colleagues, subordinates and superiors.

*The
challenge
of working
cross-
culturally*

Inevitably, tomorrow's workplace will be one of great cultural diversity. To succeed, managers will need to become expert at managing cross-cultural differences. They will need to be skilled in bringing down cross-cultural barriers that limit effective communication and interaction. Even more importantly, they will need to learn how to make cultural diversity work for them by producing something better which no one cultural approach or perspective can achieve. This is the challenge that working cross-culturally brings to each and every one of us who wishes to compete successfully in the global marketplace.

NOTES

Chapter 1: Culture at Work

Levine, Deena R., Jim Baxter & Piper McNulty, *The Culture Puzzle: Cross-Cultural Communication for English as a Second Language*, Englewood Cliffs, New Jersey: Prentice-Hall, 1987.

Hall, Edward T. & Mildred Reed Hall, *Hidden Differences: Doing Business with the Japanese*, Garden City, New York: Anchor Press, 1987.

"Minority Women Feel Racism, Sexism are Blocking Path to Management", *Wall Street Journal*, 7/25/90, p. B1.

Fernandez, John, *The Diversity Advantage*, New York: Lexington Books, 1993.

Chapter 3: The Changing Workplace

U.S. Department of Commerce, *Statistical Abstract of the United States*, Washington, D.C.: United States Government, 1992.

Fernandez, John, *The Diversity Advantage*, New York: Lexington Books, 1993.

Nelton, Sharon, "Winning with Diversity", *Nation's Business*, Vol. 80, September, 1992, p. 18-20.

Chapter 4: American Patterns of Thinking

Quote taken from a videotape of Dr. Stephen Durrant produced by the Community Services Center of Taipei, 1989.

Chapter 5: The Individualistic American

Survey by Civic Service, *Public Opinion*, June/July, 1981.

Brown, Duane & Carole W. Minor, *Working in America: A Status Report on Planning and Problems*, Washington, D.C.: National Career Development Association, 1989.

Chapter 6: The Informal American

Fieg, John Paul, *A Common Core: Thais and Americans*, Yarmouth, Maine: Intercultural Press, 1989.

Chapter 7: The Take-Charge American

Abdullah, Asma (Ed.), *Understanding the Malaysian Workforce: Guidelines for Managers*, Kuala Lumpur, Malaysia: Malaysian Institute of Management, 1992.

Milstein, Mike M., "Toward More Effective Meetings", *The 1983 Annual for Facilitators, Trainers and Consultants*, San Diego: University Associates, 1983.

Chapter 8: The Change-Oriented American

Feinsilber, Mike & William Mead, *American Averages*, New York: Doubleday & Co., 1980.

Chapter 10: Communicating With Americans

Harris, Phillip R. & Robert T. Moran, *Managing Cultural Differences*, Houston: Gulf Publishing Co., 1991.

Fieg, John Paul, *A Common Core: Thais and Americans*, Yarmouth, Maine: Intercultural Press, 1989, p. 42.

Books for Asian Readers Interested in Learning More about Americans

Althen, Gary, *American Ways*, Yarmouth, Maine: Intercultural Press, 1988.

Baldrige, Letitia, *Complete Guide to Executive Manners*, New York: Rawson Associates, 1985.

Engholm, Christopher, *When Business East Meets Business West*, New York: John Wiley and Sons, Inc., 1991.

Hall, Edward T. & Mildred Reed Hall, *Understanding Cultural Differences*, Yarmouth, Maine: Intercultural Press, 1990.

Kearny, Edward N., & Mary Ann Kearny & Jo Ann Crandall, *The American Way: An Introduction to American Culture*, Englewood Cliffs, New Jersey: Prentice Hall Regents, 1984.

Lanier, Allison, *Living in the U.S.A.*, Yarmouth, Maine: Intercultural Press, Inc., 1988.

Levine, Deena R., Jim Baxter & Piper McNulty, *The Culture Puzzle: Cross-Cultural Communication for English as a Second Language*, Englewood Cliffs, New Jersey: Prentice-Hall, 1987.

Stewart, Edward C., *American Cultural Patterns*, Yarmouth, Maine: Intercultural Press, 1972.

Wanning, Esther, *Culture Shock! USA*, Singapore: Times Books International, 1991.

Bibliography

Abdullah, Asma (Ed.), *Understanding the Malaysian Workforce: Guidelines for Managers*, Kuala Lumpur, Malaysia: Malaysian Institute of Management, 1992.

Abdullah, Asma, "Local Values in Malaysian Managerial Practices: Some Implications for Communicating, Leading and Motivating the Malay Workforce," *Intan Management Journal*, Vol. 1, (1), 1992, p. 27-63.

Acuff, Frank L., *How to Negotiate Anything with Anyone Anywhere Around the World*, New York: American Management Association, 1993.

Adler, Nancy J., *International Dimensions of Organizational Behavior*, Boston: PWS-Kent Publishing Co., 1991.

Althen, Gary, *American Ways*, Yarmouth, Maine: Intercultural Press, 1988.

Baldrige, Letitia, *Complete Guide to Executive Manners*, New York: Rawson Associates, 1985.

Berk, Joseph & Susan Berk, *Managing Effectively*, New York: Sterling Publishing Co., Inc., 1991.

Berry, John W., Ype H. Poortinga, Marshall H. Segall & Pierre R. Dasen, *Cross-Cultural Psychology: Research and Applications*, New York: Cambridge University Press, 1992.

Bond, Michael Harris, *Beyond the Chinese Face*, Hong Kong: Oxford University Press, 1991.

Brislin, Richard W., Kenneth Cushner, Craig Cherrie & Mahealani Yong, *Intercultural Interactions: A Practical Guide*, Beverly Hills, California: Sage Publications, 1986.

Brown, Duane & Carole W. Minor (Eds.), *Working in America: A Status Report on Planning and Problems*, Washington, D.C.: National Career Development Association, 1989.

Chambers, Kevin, *Asian Customs and Manners*, New York: Meadowbrook, 1988.

Christopher, Robert C., *The Japanese Mind*, New York: Simon & Schuster, 1983.

Condon, John C., *With Respect to the Japanese: A Guide for Americans*, Yarmouth, Maine: Intercultural Press, 1984.

Cooper, Robert & Nanthapa Cooper, *Culture Shock, Thailand*, Singapore: Times Books International, 1986.

Copeland, Lennie & Lewis Griggs, *Going International: How to Make Friends and Deal Effectively in the Global Marketplace*, New York: Random House, 1985.

Copeland, Lennie, "Managing in the Melting Pot," *Across the Board*, Vol. 23 (6), 1986, p. 52-59.

Crane, Paul S., *Korean Patterns*, Seoul: Kwangjin Publishing Co., 1978.

Dawson, Raymond, *Confucius*, New York: Hill & Wang, 1982.

Engholm, Christopher, *When Business East Meets Business West*, New York: John Wiley and Sons, Inc., 1991.

Feinsilber, Mike & William Mead, *American Averages*, New York: Doubleday & Co., 1980.

Fernandez, John, *The Diversity Advantage*, New York: Lexington Books, 1993.

Fieg, John Paul, *A Common Core: Thais and Americans*, Yarmouth, Maine: Intercultural Press, 1989.

Fung, Yu-Lan, *A History of Chinese Philosophy*, Princeton, New Jersey: Princeton University Press, 1952.

Gochenour, Theodore, *Considering Filipinos*, Yarmouth, Maine: Intercultural Press, 1990.

Goodman, Alan, "Intercultural Training of Japanese for U.S. - Japanese Interorganizational Training," *International Journal of Intercultural Relations*, Vol.16, 1992, p. 195-215.

Graham, J. & Herberger, R., "Negotiators Abroad — Don't Shoot from the Hip," *Harvard Busness Review*, July-August, 1983.

Hall, Edward T. & Mildred Reed Hall, *Hidden Differences: Doing Business with the Japanese*, Garden City, New York: Anchor Press, 1987.

Hall, Edward T. & Mildred Reed Hall, *Understanding Cultural Differences*, Yarmouth, Maine: Intercultural Press, 1990.

Hall, Edward T., "The Silent Language in Overseas Business," *Harvard Business Review*, Vol. 38 (3), 1960, p. 87-96.

Harris, Philip R. & Robert T. Moran, *Managing Cultural Differences*, Houston: Gulf Publishing Company, 1991.

Hildebrant, Herbert W., "Cultural Communication Problems of Foreign Business Persons in the United States," *Journal of Business Communications*, Vol. 13 (1), 1975, p. 13-24.

Hofstede, Geert, "The Cultural Relativity of Organizational Practices and Theories," *Journal of International Business Studies*, Fall, 1983, p. 75-89.

Hsu, Francis, *Americans and Chinese: Passage to Differences*, Honolulu: University of Hawaii Press, 1987.

Kearny, Edward N., Mary Ann Kearny & Jo Ann Crandall, *The American Way: An Introduction to American Culture*, Englewood Cliffs, New Jersey: Prentice Hall Regents, 1984.

Kovach, Kenneth, "What Motivates Employees: Workers and Supervisors Give Different Answers," *Business Horizons*, Vol. 30 (5), 1987, p. 58-65.

Lanier, Allison, *Living in the U.S.A.*, Yarmouth, Maine: Intercultural Press, Inc., 1988.

Lee, James A., "Changes in Managerial Values, 1965-1985," *Business Horizons*, Vol. 31, No. 4, 1987, p. 29-33.

Leppert, Paul, *Doing Business With the Koreans*, Chula Vista, California: Patton Pacific Press, Inc., 1987.

Levine, Deena R., Jim Baxter & Piper McNulty, *The Culture Puzzle: Cross-Cultural Communication for English as a Second Language*, Englewood Cliffs, New Jersey: Prentice-Hall, 1987.

Milstein, Mike M., "Toward More Effective Meetings," *The 1983 Annual for Facilitators, Trainers and Consultants*, San Diego: University Associates, 1983.

Reeder, John A., "When West Meets East: Cultural Aspects of Doing Business in Asia," *Business Horizons*, Vol. 30 (1), 1987, p. 69-74.

Rowland, Diana, *Japanese Business Etiquette*, New York: Warner Books, 1985.

Shorter, Peter, "Assignment America: Foreign Managers Beware," *International Management*, Vol. 40 (9), 1985, p. 93-97.

Stewart, Edward C., *American Cultural Patterns*, Yarmouth, Maine: Intercultural Press, 1972.

Triandis, H.C., R. Brislin & H. Hui, "Cross-Cultural Training Across the Individualist-Collectivist Divide," *International Journal of Business*, Vol. 12 (3), 1988, p. 269-289.

Uris, Auren, *The Executive Deskbook*, New York: Van Nostrand Reinhold Company, 1988.

Wanning, Esther, *Culture Shock! USA*, Singapore: Times Books International, 1991.

Yang, S.M., *Korean Customs and Etiquette*, Seoul: Moon Yang Gak, 1990.

Yengoyan, Aram A. & Perla Q. Makil (Eds.), *Philippine Society and the Individual: Selected Essays of Frank Lynch, 1949-1976*, Ann Arbor, Michigan: University of Michigan, Center for South and Southeast Asian Studies, 1984.

Index